DONG
MINGZHU
&
GREE

A BUSINESS AND LIFE BIOGRAPHY

Published by
LID Publishing Limited
One Adam Street, London WC2N 6LE

31 West 34th Street, 8th Floor, Suite 8004,
New York, NY 10001, US

info@lidpublishing.com
www.lidpublishing.com

A member of:

BPR
Business Publishers Roundtable

www.businesspublishersroundtable.com

Published in collaboration with the China Translation & Publishing House
(a member of the China Publishing Group Corporation)

 China Translation and Publishing House

© LID Publishing Limited, 2017
© China Translation and Publishing House, 2017

Printed in Great Britain by TJ International
ISBN: 978-1-911498-30-8

Illustration: Myriam El Jerari
Cover and page design: Caroline Li

DONG MINGZHU

& GREE

A BUSINESS AND LIFE BIOGRAPHY

BY **GUO HONGWEN**

LONDON   MONTERREY
MADRID   SHANGHAI
MEXICO CITY   BOGOTA
NEW YORK   BUENOS AIRES
BARCELONA   SAN FRANCISCO

CONTENTS

PRELUDE

Dong Mingzhu, chairwoman of Gree Electric Appliances Inc. (Gree's) and a leader of China's industrial reinvigoration, embodies many assets of a successful businesswoman. At the age of 36, when most women settle down into the comfort of a family, centred around their husband and children, she started a career from scratch. Step by step, advancing year by year, she eventually rose from an entry-level sales associate to the president of Gree Electric Appliances Inc. She is wise, bold, strong and firm. Dong Mingzhu's success and experience have given her a unique perspective, and her intellectual wealth surpasses that of her peers. Her journey serves as an inspiring note to young people and a textbook for entrepreneurs.

In May 2012 a re-election of the board of directors took place at Gree Electric Appliances Inc. This event marked a shift between the new and old higher-management executives.

Zhu Jianghong, the founder and chairman of the board of Gree Electric Appliances Inc., announced his retirement, and the 58-year-old Dong Mingzhu, then the vice-chairperson, was elected as president of Gree Electric Appliances Inc.

It was generally agreed among industry insiders that Zhu Jianghong's retirement would have a big impact on Gree. Whether or not this impact could be kept to the absolute minimum was up to his successor, Dong Mingzhu. Zhu Jianghong and Dong Mingzhu had worked together to create the 'Zhu Dong Team', which had overseen Gree's early successful period. "Gree won't succeed without Dong Mingzhu; Dong Mingzhu would not have grown into herself without Zhu Jianghong." These words spread inside Gree, as well as among the industry, which generally explained the relations among Zhu Jianghong, Dong Mingzhu and Gree. For the same reason, the former CEO of Kelon Electrical Holdings Co. Ltd., said, "It's Zhu Jianghong's fortune to have worked with Dong Mingzhu, and vice versa." It short, the Zhu Dong Team was the driving force behind Gree, which allowed the company to move forward.

With Zhu Jianghong retiring and Dong Mingzhu in office, people wondered what Gree would look like after the Zhu Dong Team broke up. In 2012 and 2013, after she took office, Dong Mingzhu provided two exciting answers. In 2012, Gree yielded an impressive revenue of 100.084 billion yuan, with a 19.84% increase year-on-year, exceeding its 100 billion yuan goal for the first time. Gree became the first electronic appliance company to reach 100 billion yuan in yearly revenue on a single electronic product. The net profit for shareholders in listed companies was 7.378 billion yuan, increasing 40.88% year–on-year.

In 2013, Gree yielded 120 billion yuan, with an increase of 19.90% year-on-year. The net profit for shareholders in listed companies was 10.8 billion, increasing 46.53% year-on-year; earnings per share amounted to 3.6 yuan, increasing 45.75% year-on-year.

Who could have imagined that the Haili Air Conditioning Company (as it was previously known) would grow to become the goliath that is Gree? From a revenue of less than 30 million yuan to now 120 billion yuan, Gree has become a giant 4,000 times its original size. While the yearly revenue has grown from 30 million yuan to 120 billion yuan, Dong Mingzhu has also grown from an ordinary salesperson at the Haili Air Conditioning Company to the chairperson and president of Gree. She, like the company itself, has transformed from a small fish to hit the big time.

Dong Mingzhu created the myths of marketing in China and gained massive success in a widely male-dominated business world. With her undying charisma she is an extraordinary woman and in the words of people inside the industry: "She is a maverick, observant of rules and regulations. She embraces feminine tenderness as well as the iron hand." She mercilessly subverted the established rules set by men, built a new land in a previously unknown arena, and forged a marketing myth that has astounded the world.

From the moment she set foot in Gree, Dong Mingzhu embarked on a new journey. The unusual trajectory took her name from obscurity and thrust her into the limelight. Eventually, Dong Mingzhu became chief of the biggest household air conditioning brand in the world.

Dong Mingzhu's accomplishments have won her admiration from women, and veneration and fascination from men.

She works tirelessly in pursuit of a pure ideal and sticks to her principals, while also defying implicit industry rules. She dares to challenge conventions, conceives and builds her own distribution channels, and continually forges her own path.

Dong Mingzhu sails through the business world, confident all the time, dominating her battles in business. She is stubborn and, as long as she upholds a belief, no one can convince her to the contrary. To protect the interests of the company, she turned against her own brother; to enforce a new regulation, she risked her job to confront the leaders. She is tough, never tolerating any disputes from distributors. Everything must go her way. All of these features combined illuminate Dong Mingzhu's character, revealing a woman with no equal.

Although dubbed the 'Iron Lady', Dong Mingzhu's true nature is tender and sentimental. She never wears business suits and says she dislikes them for their "serious and stubborn" effect, preferring fashionable clothes instead. When meeting with a sick child from a poor family, she generously loosens her purse strings, helping with money or goods. And, as with all mothers, her eyes sometimes become misty when talking about her son.

Dong Mingzhu's success is built upon persistence, faith and an indomitable pursuit of her dreams. In the material world, where people can be impetuous and money is everything, she fights to achieve her goals, an explicit manifestation of her noble beliefs and vision. You can feel energy and confidence radiating from her at all times; two vital elements, in part responsible for the great rejuvenation of the Chinese nation and the pursuit of the Chinese Dream. Dong Mingzhu's success shows that women can bring tenderness and beauty to the world of business and make the world vibrant and colourful.

CHAPTER

1

THE ROSE OF IRON, BEAUTIFUL AND REFINED

SELF-RELIANT AND STRIVING FOR THE BEST

In August 1954, Dong Mingzhu was born to an ordinary family in Nanjing. By order of birth, she was the seventh child. In a family not shy of children, Dong Mingzhu was the 'unwanted extra' in her parents' eyes.

When her parents named her, they picked the character 'zhu', which means pearl. At the time, her parents could not imagine their little girl's name would become synonymous with the city of Zhuhai in South China. In the same way that the adult Dong Mingzhu lights up the Gree brand with her courage and wisdom, the brand shines a spotlight on Zhuhai and illuminates the whole industry in China and the world.

Dong Mingzhu was born close to the fifth anniversary of the founding of the People's Republic of China, and a new energy and sense of reinvigoration could be felt everywhere. Her early home was Nanjing, Jiangsu, a historic city with a deep cultural heritage. Despite being the youngest of seven children, Mingzhu did not grow to be a shy or reserved child. At home, Dong Mingzhu never played the 'youngest card' to receive special treatment or indulgence from her parents or brothers and sisters. Never bratty or petty, she acted like a miniature adult even in childhood. She still likes Nanjing, the ancient city, and her childhood was immersed in it, steeped in its historic and cultural nurture. In her mind, however, Nanjing was missing an unknown something. She often went beyond the city walls to see what could be found, and each time she made new discoveries and found new inspirations.

One day Dong Mingzhu said to her mother, "The city of Nanjing looks too old. We should decorate it and make it fresh looking." Her mother told her, "That is grown ups' business. By no means should it worry you, a child. As a girl, you only need to learn to focus on your husband and children." Dong Mingzhu refuted, "Why is this men's business exclusively? Why can't women do it or talk about it?" Her mother answered, "You are too young. After you grow up, you will see my point." Dong Mingzhu remembered those words.

Dong Mingzhu was a bright, confident and stubborn child, gritty in nature. "Do what you want to do and do your best at it" is still her policy. She recalled: "In school I was never criticized by my teachers, nor had my parents been called to my school because of my discipline. I would ace all the courses and brought home a beautiful transcript at the end of each term."

Dong Mingzhu's way of doing homework was to think well before taking action, never going back to revise or make corrections. She recounted: "I never tore one page out of my notebook, which was almost flawless. Teachers would use it to set an example for other students, which, in turn, motivated me to be more careful and perfect with my homework."

Even during her school years, Dong Mingzhu knew the value of time and the crime of wasting it. After she learned something, she would never go back to review it. She recalled: "I only studied in school. After school I would never read textbooks. To go over what you already know is a waste of time to me. After school I would play sports or go hiking. As long as my grades satisfied my teachers and parents, I thought there was no need to stare at textbooks all day long."

In junior high school, the two things Dong Mingzhu wanted the most were to learn how to swim and ride a bike, both of which her parents strongly opposed. In their eyes, learning to swim or ride a bike could be unsafe, and there was no need for her to take risks. However, Dong Mingzhu insisted, and her parents had no choice but to let her. She was only 11 or 12 at that time and recalled years later: "Maybe that's who I am. I will never simply accept my failures. If I failed, I would spare no effort to change the situation until it became a success. Unyielding and self-reliant is my nature. I would never stop until I secured it." This unyielding nature leaves its mark on all aspects of Dong Mingzhu's life.

In July 1975, Dong Mingzhu graduated with honours from the Wuhu Institute of Cadre Education with a major in statistics. She was assigned to take a management job as a cadre in a chemical research institute in Nanjing, where she continued her exemplary performance. She said, "I am assiduous in nature and exert myself in my work all the time. When the leader gave me a task with a three-day deadline, I would normally end up completing it in one day and using the next two to make meticulous adjustments. I reminded myself that everything of my hand must be the best." This made Dong Mingzhu noble, elegant and continually believe in herself.

In the air conditioning industry in China, whether speaking to media professionals or business insiders, Dong Mingzhu is always spoken of as stubborn, tough and imperious. Perhaps Dong Mingzhu has solidified a certain reputation in people's minds. In the media, people see a tough and unrelenting personality. When you meet Dong Mingzhu in person, however, she shatters all of those stereotypes. Many people can't help but ask, "Are you Dong Mingzhu?" when they first meet her, because they find she is by no means short of tenderness, especially when away from her work.

Dong Mingzhu also likes embroidery and is very skilful herself. In her old house in Nanjing, all the curtains and tablecloths were designed and embroidered by her hand. Whenever talking about embroidery, a smile crinkles the corner of her eyes. She is an ordinary woman, loving beauty and fashion and made of flesh and bones.

In a corner of her office, you can see a picture of her clothed in a dark blue, sleeveless, striped dress and a pair of white sneakers, crouching down on a stone in the midst of a stream and splashing water with her hands, her face beaming into full blossom. Beautiful memories like this are so precious and memorable for Dong Mingzhu. On her desk are a few other frames containing her glamorous private pictures. She loves taking pictures and swaps new pictures into her frames when they exceed a new standard of glamour compared with the ones previously in their stead.

Dong Mingzhu is also a big fan of movies and various soap series. Regardless of the genre, she watches these shows with great scrutiny, when time allows. She continually talks about the Korean soap series *Autumn in My Heart* with people close to her. Rarely does she talk about her family, except for her son. Her cell phone wallpaper is a picture with him.

As the president and CEO of Gree, Dong Mingzhu still dresses the way she likes. An article of clothing will never be seen twice in conferences, public occasions, or on camera. In the male-dominated household electronics industry, Dong Mingzhu's grace easily distinguishes her from men in business suits. In her precious spare time, Dong Mingzhu goes shopping in outlets with great gusto. She revels in discovering gems among the array of collections, and she loves finding a bargain, even though it is obvious that Dong Mingzhu is not short of money.

Though depicted as tough and domineering, Dong Mingzhu is addressed as 'Sister Dong' inside Gree. As a distributor commented, "Dong Mingzhu has a sharp tongue, but she means well." People at Gree know that her tough persona is all for work. She sets a high standard and hides her softer side. An occasional slip of her mask surprises and delights colleagues. As Dong Mingzhu's boss and business partner for many years, the former chairman and president of Gree, Zhu Jianghong's comments have some authority: "She is a good woman, but her tongue will never surrender." Her colleagues say the same thing: "Sister Dong is tough in speech, yet soft-hearted in her core." Perhaps people inside Gree can feel her gentle heart under the veneer of an iron hand.

In the air conditioner market, Dong Mingzhu has turned Gree into the industry leader for the past 18 years. A hugely successful businesswoman, Dong Mingzhu remains composed and powerful. At the mention of her son, however, Dong Mingzhu is moved to tears. She has been busy trotting north and south, with no time to take care of her son. She thinks that over the years she has neglected him, rendering her unqualified as a mother.

In 1982, to the delight of Dong Mingzhu, her son Dongdong was born. But after just two years, her life was struck with misfortune: her husband died, leaving her and their two-year-old son behind. Strong in nature, Dong Mingzhu endured this sudden strife and withstood what life exerted on her and her son. Still, she held hopes and desires for a better life in her heart.

When the 36-year-old Dong Mingzhu left Nanjing to start up in Shenzhen, her son Dongdong was only in second grade. To pursue her dreams, Dong Mingzhu hardened her heart and gave her eight-year-old son Dongdong to her mother to care for. After she started at Gree, she only saw her son when she was on business trips to her hometown. Her son was quiet every time she was home, clinging to her like a timid kitten, as if his mother would run away if he didn't clasp her tightly.

One Sunday, Dong Mingzhu had just left the house when she found she had left important documents behind. She turned back promptly. When she passed her son's room, she went in out of curiosity and turned over his quilt. Unexpectedly, her son was weeping under the cover of the quilt, his chest convulsing with tears and snot streaming down his face. She realized at that moment, as a mother, she had not given enough to her son and had not fulfilled her duty as a mother. Dongdong, on the other hand, seeing she was back, wiped his eyes and reassured her: "Mom, please go to work. I am fine, seriously."

For the convenience of work, Dong Mingzhu sent her son to boarding school when he was 11. She hoped her son would grow up to be independent and ambitious in such an environment.

When Dongdong was 12, he completed the journey from Zhuhai to Guangzhou and then flew back to Nanjing all by himself. Two days before departure, Dongdong asked his mother, "Can you take me to the airport?" Dong Mingzhu had become a powerful businesswoman by that time, able to fulfil such requests for her son with no concern for her finances or time. Dongdong stared at her ardently, but she turned him down with a simple explanation: "Mom is busy." Dongdong asked again if she could send her colleagues to see him off, which incurred another blunt refusal. Years later, when Dong Mingzhu recalled this event, she couldn't stop panicking. She denied her son ruthlessly on such a basic request. She admits her cruelty in that incident, when her son was only 12.

In her son's growth, the lack of physical care and discipline was compensated for by continuous open conversations and advice. She always encouraged her son to be strong and independent from the time he was little. She told him that was the only way to make him competent and valuable to society.

Dong Mingzhu was delighted to see her son grow up to achieve such excellence. She is relieved now, since he has at this time entered into a career that suits him, and he has grown into an independent and successful man. Rather than lie and tell him that she will be home soon, she can now tell her son frankly that she will work even harder for the prospects of Gree.

FAVOURABLE FORTUNES: BEING RESOLUTE AND VIGOROUS

When Dong Mingzhu was little, her mind was innocent and full of fantasies. Initially, her dream was to become a teacher. Later, she wanted to become a soldier, protecting others in any way she could. She always endeavoured to become a valuable member of society.

In July 1975, Dong Mingzhu graduated with a degree in statistics from Wuhu Institute of Cadre Education in Anhui and started to work in a management position in a chemical research institute in Nanjing. After that, she got married and gave birth to her son, changing the course of her career to become a good wife and a good mother for

Gender bias]

her family. After the death of her husband, when she was at only 30, self-reliance dictated her life trajectory. She was not willing to be dependent or seek other people's pity. She yearned to forge ahead and create a beautiful life with her bare hands.

In 1990, Dong Mingzhu had something of a mid-life crisis and did not want to sit idly by and watch her youth trickle away. She quit her job in Nanjing, left her family and struck a living on her own in Shenzhen. Later she relocated to Zhuhai and kicked off a new journey by joining Gree.

Dong Mingzhu first joined Gree as a sales associate. Though ambitious, she behaved in a diffident manner. She was eager to adapt to a new environment and the role she played in it and spared no time, working with senior sales people bringing in roughly 3 million yuan in sales revenue. In the process, Dong Mingzhu also trained herself, through various methods, in installation, configuration, usage and maintenance, as well as negotiation with dealers. She regained confidence in the practice and stuck to the mantra of, "Nothing is insurmountable as long as you resolve to learn." She also came to learn that the commissions from sales could provide a stable life for her and her son.

During her earlier time at Gree, Dong Mingzhu used to take 40 days to collect a repudiated loan, which prompted her to rethink the relationship between the enterprise and dealers, and how to create a win-win cycle. Once a dealer requested 400,000 yuan's worth of goods and pre-paid 200,000 yuan. In this buyers' market, Dong Mingzhu accepted the harsh terms, but after she received 200,000 yuan, she only sent 200,000 worth of goods to the dealer. She knew the dealer wanted the loans, so to change the dealer's mindset, Dong Mingzhu voluntarily helped him with promotions. Those 200,000 worth of goods sold out in only a few days. Then she sent another 200,000 worth to him, which added up to the 400,000 as she had promised.

After that, many dealers abandoned the habit of buying on credit, with no loans in the region Dong Mingzhu was in charge of. In the same year, Dong Mingzhu achieved a yearly revenue of 16 million yuan, a beautiful business victory that was met with admiration and jealousy at the same time. The market in Anhui had been fully unblocked to Gree. Dong Mingzhu was assigned to the more competitive market in Nanjing, where she expanded the revenue to 36.5 million yuan within a year.

The exciting news of these sales revenues attracted the attention of Zhu Jianghong, who was the president of Gree at the time. In 1995, Dong Mingzhu returned to the headquarters of Gree in Zhuhai and was appointed as the director of the sales department. She initiated a series of drastic reforms and a created a new and dynamic department, despite its slack and lagging history. Growing up with Gree, Dong Mingzhu witnessed its transformation from a small enterprise with 20,000 products manufactured annually to a corporate behemoth with 60 million shipped each year.

It is said Gree would not be as it is without Dong Mingzhu. She does not refute this point, but also puts some weighty compliments on the importance of the quality of products and the collaborating efforts of all staff members involved. She also attributes her early success to Zhu Jianghong's trust in her. "If it were not for his good judgment and open mind, my voice as a ordinary sales associate would not have been heard." It is undeniable that Gree's success wouldn't have happened without Dong Mingzhu, and vice versa. The two names are inseparable.

TOGETHER WEATHERING THE STORM AND CREATING WONDERS

"Gree would not have succeeded without Dong Mingzhu; Dong Mingzhu would not have grown into herself without Zhu Jianghong." These words echo inside Gree and generally explain the relationships between Zhu Jianghong, Dong Mingzhu and Gree.

In Dong Mingzhu's office hangs a scroll of calligraphy: "Selflessly committed to Gree; Heroically conquering the business world." It was a gift to her for her 51st birthday in August 2005 from the chairman of Gree, Zhu Jianghong.

In 1991, 46-year-old Zhu Jianghong slowly built his Rome and came to the position of president of Gree. Gree was a small air conditioning company called Haili back then. Zhu Jianghong was meticulous and had a background in technology. He prioritized the research function after taking charge. Not long after, the quality of the product went through a full-scale change, inciting a new start for Haili air conditioners in the market.

In the same year, Dong Mingzhu's conquest in Anhui's market generated 2.4 million yuan revenue. In addition to Dong Mingzhu's competence and insight, the upgrading of air conditioner quality also served as a catalyst. In 1992, Dong Mingzhu hit another record of 16 million yuan in revenue in Anhui, shocking Gree headquarters as well as the president, Zhu Jianghong, especially when considering the revenue in the affluent area of Jiangsu was only 3 million. A shrewd businessman, Zhu Jianghong was stunned and impressed, and he immediately decided to inspect the east China market. After he arrived in Anhui, he quickly recognized Dong Mingzhu's talents in marketing and management. He was overwhelmed and could not sleep due to his excitement. He was impressed by Dong Mingzhu's strong sense of responsibility, unique ideas and shrewdness.

Zhu Jianghong immediately put Dong Mingzhu in charge of Nanjing, expecting her to blaze a trail for Gree in the highly competitive market. Dong Mingzhu matched and exceeded expectations: revenues rocketed in 1993. And with the additional revenue reaped in the Anhui market, Dong Mingzhu alone accounted for a considerable chunk of the company's yearly volume. It could be said that her hard work built Gree.

In the coming year of 1994, Gree's share of revenue in Jiangsu shot up to 160 million, finishing among the top three brands in Jiangsu, on par with Chunlan and Huabao. In the same year, Dong Mingzhu's personal track record accounted for 20% of Gree's yearly revenue.

In October 1994, Zhu Jianghong decisively called Dong Mingzhu back to headquarters to become the deputy director of the sales department. As a deputy director, she had no director to report to, but a vacant position for her to rise to quickly. Just after Dong Mingzhu took over as the deputy director, she noticed over 50 million debt on Gree's account, mostly irretrievable. Gree could not even provide evidence for this debt or trace any accountability for the missing money.

Dong Mingzhu was infuriated by this misconduct and resolved to investigate the matter. She went to Zhu Jianghong and openly requested an audience with the delegation of external finance authority. This line of enquiry was considered off limits, but Zhu Jianghong further contemplated Dong Mingzhu's request.

It stood to reason that Dong Mingzhu took the director position soon afterwards, and she fervently sought to eliminate debts and reinforced the policy of 'Payments before goods'. No debt has occurred in Gree's account since.

Dong Mingzhu said, "I hope that one day I can outperform president Zhu. I am convinced that he is waiting for that day too, but I also trust that president Zhu's vision is unparalleled. With the greatest of respect, if it were not for me when I came to restructure the sales department in 1994, Gree wouldn't be so impactful today. In a sense, president Zhu is lucky. He would have regretted it if he had not met me."

CHAPTER

HEADING SOUTH TO BUILD A CAREER

HEADING SOUTH AND JOINING GREE SALES

In 1990, a huge wave of people headed south for job opportunities. Dong Mingzhu, with her unyielding nature, quit her job in Nanjing, left her eight-year-old son with her mother and went to work for a chemical manufacturing company in Shenzhen.

Rather than testing the waters of the job market, Dong Mingzhu was determined and persistent with her decision. She knew she didn't have a lot of time for setbacks and failures at the age of 36. Such determination and grit won her many opportunities.

In the chemical research institute in Nanjing, Dong

30

Mingzhu worked in a management position, mostly dealing with personnel, compensation and benefits, or salary reforms. She still worked in the same profession in Shenzhen in enterprises.

Dong Mingzhu came to Zhuhai by chance and became captivated by the beautiful city environment. Immediately she adjusted her plans and moved to Zhuhai. Through unremitting efforts, she was hired by Haili Air Conditioning Company, the previous incarnation of Gree, and became a sales associate.

Gree was like a frail infant back then. This state-owned air conditioning company, small and unknown, had a yearly manufacturing capacity of 20,000 units, and yearly sales revenues between 20 to 30 million RMB. The sales department had just been set up, with 20 sales associates in total. In keeping with the annual sales plan, each associate needed to achieve an average sales revenue of 1 million. If they fulfilled the task, they would get 2% commission, which was about 20,000 yuan, a huge amount of money at that time, and even included a salary and expenses for business trips and PR activities.

Sales was a new profession in China. Because of the introduction of the new market economy in China, enterprises stripped off the burden of the planned economy, and relied on sales for revenue. All enterprises conformed to certain standards of sales staff selection. Salesmen needed to have volubility, a great capacity for liquor, and be smooth and slick in establishing social relationships. Saleswomen needed to be beautiful and sociable and apt for public relations. Dong Mingzhu didn't seemingly fit the pattern. She didn't touch alcohol, only drinking water at the table, and had a stubborn and principled attitude. Some customers didn't take notice of her; some senior sales staff didn't even have faith in her.

Considering the fact that Dong Mingzhu was unfamiliar with sales practices, the company paired her with a few senior staff to learn them in the Beijing and northeastern markets. Dong Mingzhu appreciated the opportunity, shadowing the senior sales associates around the business, visiting customers and checking inventory. Dong Mingzhu quickly became capable in each of these practices.

There was a big refrigerating exhibition hall in Beijing, particularly for air conditioner presentations and promotions. While visiting the hall with the senior sales associates, Dong Mingzhu was observant and conscientious while the senior associates talked about business with the exhibition manager. Many air conditioner brands were represented there, from home and abroad. The senior staff danced to the tune of the exhibition manager for more orders. In an affected, lofty manner, the manager said, "There is nothing special about your product, but don't worry. Since I am here, I guarantee your products in our exhibition hall will be sold out." In a seller's market, the manager's promise was not an exaggeration.

In six months, while working with senior staff, Dong Mingzhu had signed deals worth three million RMB, and learned every aspect of installation, configuration, usage and maintenance. More importantly, she learned how to do business with dealers of different characteristics in different places. Six months of practice built her confidence, and she was able to deeply comprehend the gist of the old adage, "Where there's a will, there's a way." She said, "A toddler is clumsy in steps; however, your first stumble in the business world is unforgettable. The effort was hard, but worthwhile. It dictated how I walked my own way out in the future." Gradually, she outgrew the stumbling phase in sales and marketing.

A WIN BECAUSE OF WISDOM AND COURAGE

In 1991, with six months of remoulding experience, Dong Mingzhu was sent to take charge of sales and marketing in the Anhui market. When she arrived in Anhui, the first challenge was not business, but a debt of 420,000 yuan.

Dong Mingzhu learned from salesmen in Hefei that a local dealer owed 420,000 yuan to Gree, but managed to defer the payment with different excuses each time Gree sent someone over. Unsure whether she would be able to collect the debt, Dong Mingzhu went to the company and walked into the manager's office. The manager, Mr Niu, was a slightly overweight, middle-aged man. Dong Mingzhu addressed him politely and started to talk about the debt. However, Mr Niu interrupted her after a few words and said, "I have a meeting to go to. Can we leave it for today?"

Dong Mingzhu went to Mr Niu's office almost every day the following week to discuss the debt and the ways in which they could recover it, but ended up with nothing. Every day, when they were about to finish work, Dong Mingzhu stood up and left, going back to her hotel depressed.

One day, before she left, she was determined to settle this matter. "420,000 is not a small amount for us. Do you have any idea how many factory workers were counting on this money to feed their families?" Mr Niu replied in disdain, "It's just 400,000. I haven't paid a penny for the 3 million in goods I owe another factory. They don't bother me every day!"

Dong Mingzhu couldn't endure his response, and yelled bluntly: "It's their business. Don't mix it with ours. Let me ask you: have you sold Gree's air conditioners? If you have, give us the money. If you haven't, give us back the products. Don't procrastinate. You can afford it. We can't." Mr Niu's roguish air was put down by Dong Mingzhu. He shifted to a grimace, and said, "Our company is tight in cash flow now. Can we wait a few days for this?"

Dong Mingzhu grasped this was an excuse and kept pressing: "Didn't you just say that you can't sell any Gree air conditioners? How is that related to your cash flow? Did you not sell the product, or do you not want to pay?" Mr Niu was rendered speechless. When Dong Mingzhu arrived at Mr Niu's office the next day, Mr Niu was not there. Dong Mingzhu didn't give up and waited in the office for him to show up.

Mr Niu could hide for a day, but not a lifetime. He finally

showed up in his office. Dong Mingzhu caught him and said, "You are even busier than the prime minister. So hard to catch sight of you."

Mr Niu chortled and acted generously: "You got me! I give up. You send 500,000 worth of more products to me. I will pay you together." Dong Mingzhu replied, "We can do that, but you need to let me check your inventory to see how much is left." Mr Niu waved his hand and said, "Those are substandard. No one wants them."

Dong Mingzhu insisted: "That's no problem. If those are substandard products, I will take them away rather than put them on the account. But you need to let me look at them first." Mr Niu said: "Okay. If you insist. But the warehouse keeper is not on duty today. Come tomorrow."

Mr Niu was at the end of his resources and accompanied Dong Mingzhu to the warehouse personally. Dong Mingzhu was shocked upon seeing the warehouse; it was like a big salvage station: different products stacked, unorganized, and most were without their packing boxes. Dong Mingzhu told Mr Niu: "I want to take these air conditioners back." Mr Niu agreed.

After the three-day weekend for the national holiday, Dong Mingzhu hired a Dongfen truck with a five-ton capacity. Dong Mingzhu scoured the warehouse for Gree air conditioners and carried them to the truck together with the help of some workers. The management of this company was chaotic; no one was there to supervise when things were carried away. Dong Mingzhu asked workers to take products of other brands, too, until she felt things on the truck were worth 420,000 RMB.

The whole factory was astounded when a truckload of

air conditioners arrived at Zhuhai, because Dong Mingzhu brought in the products as collateral to repay the debt. It knocked the socks off of everyone. Even the factory manager, Zhu Jianghong, started to pay special attention to this Nanjing woman. The debt recovery in Hefei improved Dong Mingzhu's prestige, not only at the management level in Gree, but in the industry as well.

BREAKTHROUGH IN ANHUI

The debt recovery experience in Hefei left an impression in Dong Mingzhu's mind. It was her first project after taking charge of the Anhui market. The gruelling 40 days honed her resilience, maturity and responsibility. She was ready to launch into the rest of her career.

Dong Mingzhu took a more deep and rational analysis of the situation afterwards. Goods before payment was the common practice at that time, but this way of doing business would lead her to problems time and time again, with new debt waiting. The time and energy spent on debt recovery added greatly to the cost of sales and marketing. The game was not worth the prize. She didn't want to repeat this cycle and waste resources.

The only way to get out of this situation was a reform of the cooperation pattern, to promote the new system of payments before goods: no payment, no goods. Dong Mingzhu decided to be the guinea pig for the experiment.

For more than a month, Dong Mingzhu visited almost all the cities in the area of Anhui and worked for the breakthrough in the problem of payment before goods. However, the response from most dealers when they heard this proposal was silence, followed by showing her the door. The sharp rebuff didn't discourage Dong Mingzhu. She still wore a smile when knocking on the next dealer's door. She believed in herself and approached the situation with confidence: there would be some credible dealers who were willing to accept her terms.

Her hard work finally paid off. The breakthrough was in an electronics shop in the city of Huainan. Dong Mingzhu was overjoyed. The manager of the shop was a slightly overweight, middle-aged woman. The sturdy look couldn't conceal the particular shrewdness of this businesswoman. This female manager, impressed by Dong Mingzhu's efforts and sincerity, agreed to order 200,000 worth of Gree air conditioners for a trial. If she could not sell them, the cooperation would stop immediately.

Dong Mingzhu valued this opportunity. She didn't leave the client abandoned after signing the contract, but offered long-term services to this manager. She used the same vigorous style of debt collection by visiting this manager time and time again to help her to expand the market, and pitched in promotion plans, like a good friend, to sell Gree air conditioners more quickly and make a profit.

Their hard work paid off and in the summer of 1992, the 200,000 yuan's worth of Gree air conditioners ordered by this shop sold out, much faster than any other brand. Dong Mingzhu's dedication in this deal touched the female manager. She was satisfied by Gree's star service. Soon, she made another payment for the second order.

Dong Mingzhu took advantage of the momentum to lobby other dealers with this real-life example of payment before goods. Orders came one after another in succession. This successful case became an example for other dealers. With Dong Mingzhu's unremitting efforts, many dealers got accustomed to this new payment schedule and accepted it completely.

From then on, 'Payment before goods: no payment, no goods' became the ground rules for Dong Mingzhu. She never allowed debt in her hands again, which became a unique sales practice in the electronics industry.

Dong Mingzhu achieved 2.4 million RMB sales revenue in Huainan that year, which made the stagnant Anhui market come to life. Gree dealers spoke highly of Dong Mingzhu's continuous service, and they thought it simple and free of worry to sell Gree products. Dong Mingzhu's reform had killed two birds with one stone. In the same year, Dong Mingzhu made two further triumphs in Wuhu and Tongling, and signed reliable dealerships in Hefei and Anqing.

In 1992, the sales revenue in Anhui increased further. Dong Mingzhu achieved sales of 16 million RMB by herself, accounting for 12.5% of Gree's yearly revenue. With her resourceful and down-to-earth actions, Dong Mingzhu soon established a new market in Anhui.

IMMERSED
IN NANJING

In the autumn of 1992, the president of Gree, Zhu Jianghong, noticed the contrast between the Anhui market, where Dong Mingzhu had achieved a sales revenue of 16 million RMB, and the Jiangsu market, which was characterized by a developed economy and affluent population, but in which Gree's sales revenue was only 3 million RBM.

After thorough deliberation, Zhu Jianghong decided to put the Jiangsu market in the hands of Dong Mingzhu, in the hopes that she would forge a new situation and create another thrilling "Anhui miracle" in the heated air conditioner market. Dong Mingzhu understood Zhu Jianghong's consideration and readily accepted this task.

Dong Mingzhu started to sell air conditioners in her home town, but rarely had time for her mother and son. Sometimes she only visited home when she was already nearby for business, and she barely stayed for a whole day. All her time and energy were spent on promoting the sales of air conditioners.

In a procurement conference at the end of 1992, Dong Mingzhu met the business manager from Jiangsu Hardware, Electricity, and Chemical Corporation. In Dong Mingzhu's endeavour, this company seriously inspected Gree and proposed to be the exclusive distributor of Gree in the Jiangsu province. In the proposal, it guaranteed no less than 10 million in sales revenue each year, and required 0.5% in commission on the sales over three million.

Given the unestablished brand awareness of Gree, and the business influence of Jiangsu Hardware, Electricity, and Chemical Corporation, plus the cost of the sales process, Dong Mingzhu persuaded Mr Zhu to sign the agreement. Gree even agreed to the commission; they could still make a fortune.

In December 1992, the traditional off-season of air conditioner sales, Jiangsu Hardware, Electricity, and Chemical Corporation, after signing the cooperation agreement, sent a first payment of two million RMB, which caused a little commotion. Gree had never received such a large one-time payment. From then on, the air conditioner department in Jiangsu Hardware, Electricity, and Chemical Corporation became Dong Mingzhu's second working office. Meanwhile, she waited, ready for the combat to come in the new year.

In 1993, a battle of air conditioner promotions erupted in Nanjing, much more intense than anyone could have expected. The private company, Suning, located in No. 60, Ninghai Road, with less than three years' experience, ignited the war. Before the traditional peak season of air conditioners sales, its slogan, "For a good summer, go Suning to buy an air conditioner", penetrated all media in Nanjing. An air conditioner model made by Huabao, for instance, was priced at 5,562 at Suning, which was 700 less than on the market. The advertisement had an immediate effect. Within four months, the air conditioner sales at Suning broke 90 million RMB, sweeping up 70% of the Nanjing market.

In the face of this, eight state-owned shopping malls in Nanjing came together and founded the 'Nanjing Electronics Market Coordination Commission' against sales tactics at Suning and announced: "The eight state-owned shopping malls accounted for 95% of air conditioner sales on the market." Together they owned more than 200,000 square metres of retail space, with billions in annual revenue. Some products were even 100 yuan less than they were at Suning, which posed a threat to Suning. In this price war, Dong Mingzhu was on the alert, but remained quietly on the sidelines. She refrained from interfering in the price and advertising war.

In June, the dramatic business war came to an end. As the hot weather dawned, air conditioners went out of stock. The prices quietly went up in all shopping malls, including Suning. Dong Mingzhu remained calm in the shifting situation and enjoyed the perks of selling all the Gree air conditioners at the regular price. Many business owners were appalled by this result.

In 1993, Dong Mingzhu brought the sales revenue in Nanjing to 36.5 million RMB, 11 times that of Jiangsu

Province in the previous year. From then on, Gree broke out of the passive status quo of the Jiangsu market. Dong Mingzhu had opened up a large market for Gree. In 1994, Dong Mingzhu achieved a sales total of 160 million, accounting for one fifth of Gree's revenue.

RESISTING TEMPTATION AND ENTRUSTED IN CRISIS

A shift occurred as the seasons changed. At the end of autumn in 1994, a 'collective resignation' of key sales employees took place at Gree, which pulled the rug out from under its feet. At that time, a company located in Zhongshan, Guangdong, promised the vice-president of Gree that once sales revenue exceeded 30 million RMB, the salesman would be granted 3% on all sales over 30 million RMB to use for business operations, and 2% for advertisement, which was almost ten times Gree's reward standard. This tantalizing offer led the major forces in Gree's sales department to leave for this other company, seeking profit, and led to a reckless collective resignation.

The president of Gree, Zhu Jianghong, felt this sudden change deeply; the success of an enterprise needed a united team. The enterprise should take care of its employees and win their sincerity in return. The enterprise needed to discover and develop talented people with its own organization. Only people who couldn't be poached were the employees who were truly needed. Those who stayed through the crisis became the backbone of the enterprise.

The collective resignation of Gree's sales group was not an accident in the competitive and unregulated air conditioner market. Some enterprises simply attributed their accidental success to a first-class salesman, rather than the overall effort of the enterprise, and plotted to poach good sales staff at any cost.

Dong Mingzhu showcased her capability during this crisis and was promoted to director of the sales department by Zhu Jianghong. The salary for sales associates soared in the poaching practice. Someone offered a yearly salary of 2 million RMB to Dong Mingzhu, which would have been a temptation for anyone.

The collective resignation made sense, due to the lucrative temptation from the company in Zhongshan. Dong Mingzhu was not tempted at that time. On the contrary, she became more determined to stay with Gree and Zhu Jianghong. She felt a lot of gratitude towards Gree and Zhu Jianghong, and she would not forget it.

The collective resignation had a big impact on the daily operations of Gree and the whole industry. In November 1994, Gree organized the procurement for 1995 at the Zhuhai Hotel, and gathered hundreds of distributors at the event. Yet, on the second day, the company from

Zhongshan organized another procurement, where 11 former Gree employees – including the former vice-president, eight Gree salesmen and two financial workers – showed up and brought another 300 distributors, out of which 340 had attended Gree's procurement event the day before. Suddenly, everyone at Gree felt jittery in the face of this adverse situation, which seemed unmanageable.

After that incident, Zhu Jianghong realized the significance of the construction of a stable, middle-level team of cadres. Since the problem occurred in the sales department, the priority was to rebuild the management team of the sales department.

Zhu Jianghong decided to promote from within by election. A poll was carried out, including different aspects of teamwork, working capability, organizational and management skills, and comprehensive performance. The poll showed Dong Mingzhu was the leader in most categories, as she had had top yearly evaluations for a few years running.

In the internal election, Dong Mingzhu was entrusted with the director's position in the sales department at this critical moment, and she was about to lead this traumatic enterprise in finding a rescue strategy.

In October 1994, Dong Mingzhu ended her three years as a sales associate and readied herself for a new position at the company headquarters, where she had a simple conversation with Zhu Jianghong, explaining: "I came to this director position to do things well, not for power. If they are not for my personal interests, I hope you will back me up in all the decisions I make." Zhu Jianghong gladly accepted this request.

After Dong Mingzhu started this post, she completely overturned Gree's debt, and led the transition in sales from individual promotions to scale promotions. A new age for Gree was ushered in.

3

CHAPTER

SETTING MODELS WITH WORDS AND ACTIONS

A FIRM BELIEF THAT WOMEN ARE NOT INFERIOR

Dong Mingzhu believes the success of a woman's career depends on confidence, persistence, fortitude and dedication, which are principles and beliefs she adheres to in both her professional and personal life.

Dong Mingzhu never recognized the influence feminine characteristics had on her career, nor did she emphasize her female identity. She disliked that some women used femininity as a weapon to survive and profit in the world, and disdained the act of marrying a rich man for a better station in life rather than earning it through hard work.

To outsiders, Dong Mingzhu, who created the miracle of Gree, was mysterious. however, this is not actually the case; Dong Mingzhu is a simple and pure person. Any distributors who have done business with Dong Mingzhu know that no schematic tricks or petty shrewdness were allowed in front of Dong Mingzhu. Only a genuine attitude could win her respect and possible cooperation.

Most Chinese people are aware of the implicit rules prevalent in China, so penetrating in each industry that they often baffle foreigners. Dong Mingzhu always told the distributors: "A lot of problems that occur in our cooperation are because of implicit rules. We all know it takes two to tango, but implicit rules run rampant, because no one plays by the rules, or abides by regulations, only seeking to benefit by exploiting implicit rules." Dong Mingzhu rejected this way of conducting business. She promised cooperation on the grounds of mutual benefits and remained unswayed by sly business practices.

Once, a dealer brought 6 million in cash to Dong Mingzhu, asking her to pull some strings for the order. This was turned down by Dong Mingzhu on the spot. Dong Mingzhu told the distributor: "If I give you some favourable terms today because of 6 million RMB, I will give better terms to those who show up tomorrow with 10 million. It's unfair to you, isn't it?" Her words convinced the dealer of her frank and forthright character and the open and fair cooperation she advocated.

A fundamental belief was embedded in Dong Mingzhu's mind that one should live to serve the community; an enterprise should take on social responsibility rather than seeking profits alone.

She also said with pride that: "I had many dreams when I was in school. I deemed teaching a noble profession, because they bring out talent in people; I regarded doctors as great, because they save lives; I also respected soldiers, because of the unyielding and just air in them. Those are three noble professions in my mind. Now, I feel I have achieved all three dreams as the manager of Gree."

Gree's employees talked about Dong Mingzhu in private: "In fact, she is unfortunate. She never gets enough rest, has no time for doctors or sickness. She is alone all the time, with no one to accompany her after work." They all knew that this successful woman had dedicated all her time and energy to the development of Gree.

Dong Mingzhu would take business trips alone all the time. However, she didn't like to eat in fancy restaurants or stay at fancy hotels. Instead, this thrifty person was always striving to improve the salaries of her employees. As early as 2006, Dong Mingzhu proposed to improve the base salary of the basic level employees to above 30,000 yuan a year. As Dong Mingzhu was fighting for her ideals, she harvested more than personal glory and the success of Gree; she also won enormous respect from wider society.

TOUGH ACTIONS WIN THE RESPECT OF EMPLOYEES

The success of the business that Dong Mingzhu oversaw can be attributed to many different factors, but the fundamental one was business management. Marketing and sales were of course crucial, but not as crucial as the role business management played. Good marketing and sales strategy cannot work under a bad management system. As a mature air conditioner brand, Gree was tested in a competitive and unpredictable market. Its success could be attributed to its marketing and sales, as well as industry-leading technology and management.

Dong Mingzhu trusted her business sense and intuition. Many female business professionals survive in the male-dominated business world by becoming one of them, but Dong Mingzhu tried to manage her business by utilizing her unique female perspective. She started from the bottom and worked her way up to the head manager of an enterprise with 80,000 employees, winning respect from many male entrepreneurs. Some used to fly directly to Gree to see what this woman was like, which may sound like a joke, but was surprisingly true.

Observing Dong Mingzhu at work, she has a full, clear tone, and speaks at a fast pace, revealing her confidence. Her signature style is that she may not speak up but, if she does, she does so in an impassioned and forceful manner.

She frankly admits she is too serious and stubborn at work sometimes. "I am very strict at work and don't consider the surface issues. A fault is a fault, and needs to be identified. I separated life and work clearly. Work is work, and life is life. I don't mix them together. I don't mix any tender feelings with work, which I treat as a battle. We all know that no personal feelings can solve any problem on the battlefield. We should use disciplined management and strict enforcement to solve problems at work, or we will go nowhere."

Dong Mingzhu was not only strict with employees, but with her family and relatives as well. She said, "Some dealers knew my brother and wanted more distribution through their connection with him. It would not damage Gree's interest to give that to my brother, those channelling benefits. However, I didn't do that, and instead put that dealer out of stock for half a month as punishment. My brother didn't understand me, regarding me as too cruel to family, and he didn't contact me for decades. To promote Gree's business is my lifetime pursuit, and I won't allow any misdeeds on my part."

At that time, bureaucratic dealings were rife at Gree, as in other state-owned companies, and problems of corruption and overstaffing were common. The management was in such disorder that dealers needed to bribe the office staff to get their deliveries. Some sales associates resorted to connections and bribery to pull strings for more profits. Dong Mingzhu was aware of this undercurrent and waged a battle against these misdeeds. She overrode all objections and made a rule that no accounts receivable were allowed and goods should be delivered after payments.

In her own words: "It's crucial for business leaders to have the courage to fight the status quo and the capability to analyse and solve problems. In the 20 years I have been working at Gree, I have fought with the market, the opponents and myself all the time. My harsh and strict management approach may render someone disgraced. It's unnecessary to make a fuss if someone thinks of me as domineering."

CHALLENGING THE GOVERNMENT TO FIGHT FOR EQUALITY

Dong Mingzhu was one of the few entrepreneurs in China who dared to challenge the government. Everyone knew that it would elicit a negative response, but Dong Mingzhu was determined in her defiance.

On 4 November 2008, a big day for Gree, the premier supplier candidate would be selected for the project of variable refrigerant system installations in the outpatient building of Panyu Central Hospital in Guangzhou. The project budget was as high as 22.2 billion RMB, a lucrative business venture for any air conditioning company.

In the short 14-day period, the most competitive and

anticipated project contractor, Gree, was unexpectedly defeated. The bid was won by Guangdong Petrochemical Construction Group, whose bidding price was as high as 21.51 million RMB, 4.44 million higher than Gree's. This company didn't even manufacture or sell air conditioners. It was later proved that they used Midea and Daikin air conditioners.

In bidding for the air conditioner installation project at the hospital, theoretically the bidders were confined to air conditioner manufacturers or dealers that had experience in hospital projects. However, in the bidding requirements, Panyu Central Hospital specifically added "the experience of railway, airport, port, subway or other municipal level infrastructure projects" besides "hospital projects".

Among the six selected candidates, only Gree was an air conditioning company with air conditioner installation experience. The other five were namely Guangdong Petrochemical Construction Group, Guangzhou Water Conservancy Equipment Installation Company, Chinese Construction Third Engineering Bureau, Guangzhou Fine Arts Company, and Guangdong Province Overseas Chinese Building and Decoration Company. None of them were air conditioner manufacturers or dealers. Other air conditioner companies didn't participate in the bidding. Wasn't this 20 million in business appealing to them?

In fact, the predetermined result was spread among the industry even before the bid. One day before the bid, a Gree representative received a call from another selected company to make Gree an offer for dropping out of the bid, which created the suspicion that maybe other air conditioner companies had received the same offer to drop out.

According to Panyu Central Hospital, Gree's equipment didn't meet the industry standard, so no procurement was made on it. In November 2008, Guangzhou Government Procurement Centre reviewed the case and announced that Gree wasn't qualified for the project, and Guangdong Petrochemical Construction Group was selected to be the project contractor.

With Dong Mingzhu's unyielding nature, Gree immediately filed a complaint to the Panyu District Finance Bureau, but it was rejected. Then Gree filed an administrative review application to Guangzhou Municipal Finance Bureau, which was accepted; Gree was overjoyed. On 22 April, Guangzhou Municipal Finance Bureau announced the review: the claim about Gree's product was unjust, and the evidence was deficient.

However, the positive atmosphere very soon dissipated. In a month, Panyu District Finance Bureau selected seven experts from irrelevant fields, organized a review of Gree products for the third time, and came to the same initial conclusion that Gree didn't meet the requirements for the bid, rendering the bid invalid. Gree had no choice but to file a second application for another administrative review. Unfortunately, in the following September Guangzhou Municipal Finance Bureau announced its decision to maintain the decision of the Panyu District Finance Bureau.

On 23 November 2009, Gree filed government procurement civil proceedings, taking Guangzhou Panyu Central Hospital and the Guangzhou Government Procurement Centre to court for their misdeed in the illegal bidding, and demanded compensation of 63,862.31. When asking compensation of only 60,000 yuan in a deal worth more than 12 billion, an ulterior motive seemed evident.

In 31 December, however, Tianhe District Court dismissed the motion on the grounds that the Guangzhou Municipal Finance Bureau was not the proper defendant in the case. As for the action to "challenge the government", Dong Mingzhu had a specific motivation. In fact, Gree was on the same side as the government. Gree wasn't targeting anyone in particular, but hoped for a just and new era of transparent operations in the government procurement system.

OPENING PATHS BY COUNTERING CONVENTIONS

People knew Dong Mingzhu was more than a wild card. Until today, many practices of abandoning conventions and establishing new patterns were connected with Dong Mingzhu directly or indirectly. She always knocked the socks off people in the industry, as they were so used to old practices. But earth-shattering changes were taking place in Gree, as well as the whole air conditioning industry.

The marketing and sales reforms in Gree had a profound impact on the status quo of the air conditioning industry. The reformer was the sales queen of Gree, Dong Mingzhu, who also initiated incredible changes in each aspect of Gree's operations with her professional prescience and personal charisma.

Some professionals in the industry started to study the 'Dong Mingzhu phenomenon', and proposed a series of questions: "Was her aptitude in marketing innate or learned? Why couldn't other people become a successful salesperson like her, even after studying books and cases?"

Gree had more than 80,000 employees, but those internal relationships were not complicated at all. In most Chinese enterprises, state-owned or private, complications with personnel were always a bigger issue than market expansion, which made Gree's situation more ideal in contrast. Dong Mingzhu worked as a mid-level management executive and vice-president for a long time and so understood the best way to deal with these issues.

As Dong Mingzhu was the head of the sales department, she made a rule stating that there was to be no food during work time, with the punishment of 50 yuan for those who broke the rule once, 100 yuan for twice, with the third time resulting in termination of employment. People in the sales department took it as merely talk, rather than serious policy. One day, when Dong Mingzhu walked into the office, she caught sight of eight employees eating snacks and fined each of them 50 yuan, even though it was only ten minutes away from the end of the work day. Dong Mingzhu told them that any rule she made would be executed stridently. If someone broke it, even in the smallest matter, they would need to face the consequences.

Back then there was a tricky situation in the sales department. Many people joined Gree through connections to senior managers. Even their direct supervisors didn't dare to manage those people. Dong Mingzhu didn't care about this, however, and was determined to regulate those people and create a transparent sales department.

An employee with just such connections was in charge of making sales plans and writing invoices. He had some power and was defiant of company regulations. Dong Mingzhu began to keep an eye on him. Not long after, she found his account was incorrect, affecting millions' worth of product deliveries. Dong Mingzhu punished him severely for this by reducing his base salary and circulating a notice of criticism throughout the company.

Unexpectedly, Dong Mingzhu received a call from the vice-president on the second day after issuing this punishment. She was called to the upstairs office and questioned on her authority for such punishment of employees. Dong Mingzhu argued, stating her reasons: "He made 5 million RMB disappear from the company's account. Is that 100 yuan fine too much for him? If I had the power, I would fire him."

The vice-president was rendered speechless by Dong Mingzhu's argument, and switched to a gentler tone to suggest a written warning for punishment instead. However, Dong Mingzhu did not yield. She told this vice-president outright: "I punished him for your concern. I could turn a blind eye to it and be a gentle person with colleagues for my personal benefit. However, if I consider it from the company's perspective, I need to punish him, for his misconduct brought shame on your reputation." The vice-president didn't know how to reply to this and let it go.

ESTABLISHING BRAND VALUE BY CREDIBILITY

Dong Mingzhu has often said that to manage an enterprise and to sell a product starts from being an honest and trust-worthy person. Only that kind of person is able to create an enterprise with credibility and a product with a good reputation. In an organization, each person and each department needs to conform to the practice of 'good people before good products', and be aware that 'every person represents the company's image; and everyone builds the sales environment'. Sales personnel on the front line, in particular, represent of the image and culture of the company and need to work hard to ensure the honour and credibility of the company.

In 2013, as part of 'Credibility Builds Up the Business', organized by central government ministries – including the Ministry of Commerce, the Propaganda Department of the Central Committee of the CPC, the National Development and Reform Commission, and the Ministry of Industry and Information Technology – the first 'credible enterprises list' was published by CCTV network, which included 20 national enterprises as the 'model enterprise for credibility' Gree was selected as a model enterprise for credibility as the representative from the electronics industry.

Dong Mingzhu was convinced that a dishonourable person had no future, nor did a dishonourable nation or enterprise. Credibility was priceless; neither people nor enterprise could survive without it. Credibility was the principle of businessmen from ancient times, the foundation of sustainable business development, and the key to winning the market. No company could go far without it.

Dong Mingzhu did a serious analysis of brands that had quickly boomed and quickly vanished, and drew the conclusion that they were abandoned by customers for a fatal weakness in the business ethical code: the lack of basic credibility.

Dong Mingzhu believed credibility was the cornerstone of brand value. The brand would be hollow without it. Entrepreneurs needed to incorporate credibility into the brand value to earn a good reputation and achieve sustainable development. 'Great air conditioner, Gree brand', was more than an advertisement. It embodied the core value of Gree.

Gree was endeavouring to protect the dealers' interests all the time. Whether or not they promoted a certain brand depended on the product quality. Some businesses were in for the long haul, while others for the short. Dealers always cared about long-term interests.

Dong Mingzhu understood the significant influence dealers had over product promotion. While she valued the market as a priceless treasure, she considered the dealers as the ones who spun the web of the market. Dong Mingzhu believed in two key points: good product quality and a good relationship with dealers.

Many dealers and suppliers were gathered on each end of Gree's supply chain. Whether or not Gree could build honest partnerships with them foretold their growing potential. In the competitive electronics market, the relationship with suppliers and dealers could predict a company's future.

Dong Mingzhu said that if there was a secret to Gree's marketing strategy, it was the rule of equal cooperation, with no tricks, with the same goal of legal business profits. That explained the emergence of the 'self-built distribution channel' and the 'regional sales company' at Gree.

As they say, the proof of the pudding is in the eating and, by 2013, Gree had achieved the top sales revenue in the world for air conditioning companies for eight years consecutively, and for 18 years in China. It created an unbelievable user base, as big as 25 million. Its pursuit of business ethics, quality and justice built a model for the industry and promoted positive practices as well.

As Dong Mingzhu said herself: "The competition among enterprises could be boiled down to competitions of brand and credibility. The product had a life cycle, but the vitality and influence of a brand could be endless. Credibility is the core for the survival and development of a business, and can't be touched. Credibility was the essence for brands more than 100 years old, and it was the priority for Gree to forge a reputable brand."

CHAPTER 4

FULFILLING TASKS, FEARLESSLY AND SELFLESSLY

ASKING TO DELEGATE POWER IN HER NEW POST

After the collective resignation incident, Dong Mingzhu took the bull by the horns and became director of the sales department. She didn't want to see the career she had devoted so much to fall to stagnation and so challenged herself to acquiesce to the company and people who had supported her through hard work.

After the hit caused by the collective resignation, Dong Mingzhu considered limiting the power of sales staff to an appropriate amount. Sales associates were employees, working for salary and commission. The dealers were not employees, but made profits on the sales of Gree air conditioners. From this perspective, sales associates and dealers were in the same boat as Gree. With some strategy, it was not impossible to make dealers an extension of Gree's business, which would take the place of and the role of the sales department. The theory was that it would improve both management and sales.

To better manage the disparate sales team, Dong Mingzhu made a rule: Gree sales staff were not allowed to earn any commission from dealers. Whoever broke this rule, no matter how small the amount, would be fired. She also designed a worksheet for salespeople. They needed to fill in the details of the time, place and people involved and the content of conversations for each business transaction. The worksheets needed to be handed in and kept by the company as evidence to undergo inspection. Very soon, a well-managed, well-trained, and compendious sales team was formed at Gree.

To eradicate the act of abusing the company's trust for private interests, Dong Mingzhu did an unbelievable thing and requested outright control of finances from the president, Zhu Jianghong. The reasoning behind this was the close connection between sales and finance. She required payment before goods, but it was only clear to the finance department whether or not clients had sent the money to the account or how much they had sent.

The current management system resulted in some clients unable to get delivery after their payments and others getting the goods before paying. Before each delivery, each invoice writer from the sales department needed to check whether the dealer had sent the money. But people in the finance department always replied, "We need to check accounts for that." In this fashion, no matter how hard sales staff worked, any slight non-cooperation with the finance department would disturb the whole operation. If it went on like this, Gree might fall back to a state of overlapping functions and unclear delegation of responsibilities.

Zhu Jianghong asked Dong Mingzhu directly: "You have asked to participate in finance management, but who will supervise you?" Dong Mingzhu replied without hesitation: "Anyone can supervise me. They can check on the account at any time. I didn't ask for the authorization to spend money as I like. I just want to be informed of whether or not dealers have made their payments so I can proceed with the delivery process in a timely manner. If it is inconvenient for me to participate in the financial management, I need the finance department to check on the dealers' payments every day and report to the sales department."

Dong Mingzhu was succinct and precise with Zhu Jianghong, and he understood that she wasn't attempting to increase her power, but sought more efficient operations at Gree. Zhu Jianghong thought that if he didn't back Dong Mingzhu up on this, she might not keep working for Gree. He therefore granted her request.

It was sacrilege to ask for this delegation of power. She was a wild card, breaking traditions, but the power became magic in Dong Mingzhu's hands. She set up a cyclical credit monitoring system: project planners were supervised by finance staff, the finance staff by invoice writers, invoice writers by computer systems, and computer systems by project planners.

"Power means responsibility," Dong Mingzhu said. "With more power, one should take more responsibility and also the courage to challenge the status quo. My power came from Gree, so I used it to serve Gree."

SHOULDERING RESPONSIBILITY AND ACTING PROMPTLY

In 1995, a fire broke out in a labour training centre in Hainan, and cost more than 300,000 yuan in losses. The cause was investigated and attributed to a malfunction of Gree air conditioners. The training centre spread the news that they were going to take Gree to court. It was the prime season for the air conditioner market, and Gree's management decided collectively to settle this issue out of court.

To reach a settlement, Gree paid 320,000 yuan to the labour training centre in compensation. In the settlement deal, the tone was "Gree electronics was responsible for the fire".

In 1996, Dong Mingzhu had just been promoted to

director of the sales department, and it was the first busy season for air conditioner sales under her management. Unbelievably, the labour training centre in Hainan had another fire, and again attributed the cause to Gree's products, requesting a compensation of 1 million yuan.

Gree immediately called an urgent meeting of management executives and discussed solutions. Any mishandling of the matter would discredit the brand's reputation in the market. If the media reported it, sales revenues in the critical peak season would decline. It was necessary for the management executives to sit together and discuss this.

Dong Mingzhu still had pent-up anger about this issue from the previous year. She didn't expect that they would play the same trick again this year for money. She was outraged. In the previous year, she didn't have the power to deal with it, but now it was under her management.

Dong Mingzhu spoke up, and proposed to deal the lawsuit. "We need to investigate this ourselves first," she said. "If it's our fault, we will pay the compensation sincerely. If it's not our fault, and they tried to rip us off, we won't pay anything. They had a fire last year, and again this year. If we keep paying for their silence, they may have a fire next year as well." Dong Mingzhu's words impressed everyone on the spot and embarrassed those leaning towards the idea of settlement. It was decided at the meeting that Dong Mingzhu would take charge of solving this issue.

In a sweeping manner, Dong Mingzhu sent out a few Gree delegates to the labour training centre in Hainan to keep an eye on them. She personally called them every day for an information update and to discuss strategy. The delegates followed her instructions and checked on the fire site, studied the pictures and fire department records meticulously, and came to the conclusion that the labour training centre was swindling Gree for financial gain. Gree settled this matter and issued no compensation. The training centre never had a fire again.

In the spring of 2001, Dong Mingzhu was promoted to general manager of Gree Electric Appliances Inc. of Zhuhai, which marked a revolutionary change in the company and brought the management of Gree up to the industry standard. Gree's sales revenue soared from 7 billion RMB to 23 billion RMB by 2005 and they surpassed the Korean Brand LG with annual sales of 12 billion units, becoming the biggest player in the global market.

When CCTV announced China Economic Figures of the Year of 2006, Dong Mingzhu was elected to be one of the top ten entrepreneurs of the year, one of the two female entrepreneurs who won this honour and the first representative from the air conditioning industry. She was also esteemed as "the great businesswoman who illuminated the Chinese economy", an honour both to Dong Mingzhu and Gree.

Granting this great honour upon Dong Mingzhu was not simply based on her achievements in forging a national brand. In the evaluation issued by CCTV's China Figures, Dong Mingzhu's qualities could be seen: responsibility, innovation, influence and inspiration. Compared with the standards from the previous year, they prioritized and emphasized these as the first criterion of national figures. When considering the four aspects together, it made sense that Dong Mingzhu was selected.

As an entrepreneur, Dong Mingzhu believed in honesty and cooperation, advocated innovative research with intellectual property, contributed to the community with material and spiritual wealth, and took responsibility. As a woman, she believed in gender equality in psychology, mindset and social value. She accompanied each step of Gree's development and made the first 'global brand' of the Chinese air conditioning industry.

STAYING AWAY FROM IMPETUOUSNESS AND FOCUSING ON SPECIALIZATION

Many temptations crossed Gree's path. Many refrigerator, TV and washing machine manufacturers came to Gree to ask to merge or to put Gree's name on their products. All encountered the same result: rejection.

Dong Mingzhu was never deluded by superficial impressions or short-term interests, and she was always sceptical of any fortuitous situation that landed in her lap. Dong Mingzhu said: "If the contracted manufacturers didn't innovate technology or improve product quality, they wouldn't have good sales prospects even with Gree on the label, and this may even implicate Gree itself." With regard to mergers and acquisitions, she believed she could expand if she could guarantee the other party would accept Gree's culture, but she wouldn't expand rashly.

Dong Mingzhu thought Gree needed to focus on the air conditioning market and make the best use of its advantage. In the air conditioning industry, Gree was the only brand with a singular focus on air conditioners. The brand value, vitality and capacity all rose from its specialization.

Specialization enabled Gree to achieve breakthroughs in technology and development, and granted advantages in brand promotion. Some experts had analysed the reason Gree stood out in the homogenized product market, and attributed it to the emphasis of specialization. Many customers trusted Gree because of its sole focus.

Dong Mingzhu didn't entirely agree with this analysis. Different business philosophies would cultivate different products. Dong Mingzhu considered Gree, for instance. When Gee completed its construction project, bringing new technology to the company, they had more than 120 laboratories, where different tests and damage control experiments were run on each product. Gree's products were expected to have a life expectancy of more than eight years, and no component would malfunction in that time.

Dong Mingzhu said Gree's specialization in air conditioners would persist until a replacement for air conditioners was developed. They would not speculate in broad investment. Dong Mingzhu said that time and effort were limited, diversified expansions needed the support of capital and capacity, and the corresponding managing system. Each category of product required specialized people and technology. Without the sound accumulation of technology and people, rash expansion could cost a company its life.

Dong Mingzhu also believed that in the vast, competitive market, each enterprise couldn't satisfy all the needs of customers. If all resources and energy were focused on one point to satisfy one need from customers, the enterprise laid the groundwork for survival and further development.

Gree's practice of specialization illustrated this point: to amass and integrate resources and work on one aspect was a plausible strategy for Chinese enterprises in the global competition. With one specialization, Gree put itself in the customers' shoes, and served the customers' needs all the way, considering it the means for enterprise development. This specialization strategy guaranteed the development focused on customers as the centre.

Because of specialization, Gree's products grew to cover 20 major categories of family and business models, 400 different ranges, and 7,000 different products. Gree became the air conditioner manufacturer with the biggest and most comprehensive product range.

Dong Mingzhu never hid her aspirations to build Gree into the top air conditioner brand in the world. She eventually fulfilled her dreams. In the air conditioning market, continuous market share growth in Gree was achieved by principled operations. Whether in sales and marketing, or management, Gree always pursued 'Great air conditioner, Gree brand'.

Gree was fully aware of the loopholes and risks in diversified and specialized development. Whether Gree would pursue diversified development in the future was a concern in the industry. Dong Mingzhu was not in favour of diversification. She said many times that Gree would not pursue diversification irrationally. Many different companies extended their tentacles into many areas, which could decentralize the energy and capital to grow in one area. Competition penetrated each industry and enterprise. She needed to pursue excellence in her own work to gain credentials in a competitive market.

CONFRONTING MALPRACTICE, AND NOT WORKING WITH THOSE ON A DIFFERENT PATH

In 1996, a fierce and brutal price war broke out in the domestic air conditioning market; major domestic brands competed for a lower price, so low as to close the gap between the purchasing and production costs. When Gree was considering whether or not to join this battle, Dong Mingzhu, the director of the sales department, strongly argued against chasing a low price. After serious discussion, management decided to support Dong Mingzhu's stance and not reduce the price at all.

However, a big Gree distributor, with millions of sales a year, took the opposite standpoint. This distributor accounted for about 10% of Gree's total revenue. This distributor started a partnership with Gree in the Jiangsu market in 1995 and became the biggest distributor of Gree's products within a year. The distributor became brash and announced: "Gree would agree to any policy I proposed."

After a short while, this distributor would not abide by Gree's marketing policies. He pulled strings, using his upper-level management connections, and dumped air conditioners in the cold season in over ten provinces, including Sichuan, Guangdong, Hunan, Hebei, Jiangxi, and Anhui. The price was even lower than his purchasing cost. His actions damaged Gree's market system, putting many other Gree dealers in a predicament with no sign of any profits.

In the cold summer of 1996, this distributor ordered 80 million RMB worth of Gree air conditioners to stockpile. If Gree cut the price, he could crush other Gree distributors, even at his own cost, to dominate the Jiangsu market and make Gree dependent on him there.

Usually, a distributor with such a massive capacity would conquer the manufacturer and let the issue lie, but this was not Dong Mingzhu's style. She would not succumb to the aggression, and strove to create an equal and principled sales environment for all distributors.

Dong Mingzhu cut the product supply to him, even though he had made the payments and had close connections to one of the high-level executives at Gree. He didn't reflect on his misconduct and instigated other distributors to file complaints against Dong Mingzhu at Gree headquarters in Zhuhai. They threatened to stop selling Gree's products if Gree continued Dong Mingzhu's policy.

Dong Mingzhu was not a pushover; she wouldn't make a compromise even at the risk of losing her position. She said: "If I give in and tolerate the misconduct of this distributor, Gree will lost discretion in setting the price to distributors. Without autonomy, we will not be as competitive in the market."

Dong Mingzhu's decision to get rid of this distributor appalled everyone in the sales department. It meant Gree would lose billions in sales a year. However, the shutout of unregulated distributors could protect other distributors' interests, safeguard their operation of sales, and stabilize the distributors' team and Gree's market. It was proven that Dong Mingzhu was right in her decision.

Gome used to be the most reliable distributor for Gree. In February 2004, another sales cycle started in the air conditioning market. Gome pursued quick returns and small margins, and manoeuvred the price of Gree air conditioners without authorization from Gree.

At that time, Dong Mingzhu was in Beijing for the National People's Congress (NPC). She was shocked and infuriated by this news. She believed this act crippled Gree's price system and tarnished Gree's top-line brand image. She immediately called Gree's sales manager in Sichuan and requested the termination of the act and an apology to Gree.

Gome apologized, but didn't yield in action. They immediately ordered all the malls to remove Gree air conditioners from the shelves. Dong Mingzhu wouldn't concede either. She immediately ordered to stop Gree's supplies from being sent to Gome.

They would not work with people whose way was not the same as theirs. Gree and Gome had different business philosophies: Gome was a giant of traditional distributors, conquering the market through chain stores; Gree was a revolutionary in new sales models, testing the feasibility of different channels. In the battle of these two models, Dong Mingzhu was always confident that Gree would emerge on top.

FORGING A NEW PATH TO INCORPORATE DISTRIBUTORS

When the confrontation between Gree and Gome broke out in 2004, nearly all industry experts hinted that, without the national chain store distributor, Gree was heading on the road to ruin. With hindsight, the opposite proved to be true. Two years after Gree stopped working with Gome, in 2006, the sales of many air conditioner brands began to falter on the market. All except for Gree, who kept a substantial growth against the trend and shot way ahead of other first-line brands. In that year, the sales revenue of Gree exceeded 20 billion RMB for the first time, increasing 30% year-on-year. Net profits reached 62.8 million RMB, increasing 23.88% year-on-year.

Gree proved with facts that the confrontation with Gome didn't kill them, but made them stronger. This result bewildered the media and many other enterprises. The spotlight shone on Gree, as many attempted to unveil the secret of their success.

The Gree model refers to the sales strategy and practice of Gree, which was appraised as "the new sales model of the 21st century". It made a huge impact on the industry, with different reviews of Gree. The creator of the Gree model was Dong Mingzhu, who was well known for her innovative and surprising moves.

On 20 December 1997, the Hubei Gree Air Conditioning Sales Company was officially launched. It was the first regional sales company of its kind for a particular brand founded by a manufacturer and distributors together. The operation model for this joint-stock company was the uniformity in distribution channels, sales and marketing, and product service. It cut out a unique, specialized sales channel, and a new cooperation structure where the manufacturers and distributors joined together for sales and market expansion, and shared interests and risks.

Gree's regional sales companies maximized their network of wholesalers with massive stores and abundant capital flow. Advantages of scale showed up. After the integration, Gree achieved rapid growth in sales. In 1998, the sales revenue of Gree air conditioners reached new heights, with an increase of 40%. The second distributors made lucrative profits too. The market became regulated and improved.

Dong Mingzhu's intention was clear: to bind manufacturers, distributors and customers together for common interests, rather than be locked in a price war, competing individually. All distributors were shareholders, and Gree was the controlling shareholder. With individual interests becoming the common interest, all were more disciplined in price setting and customer service.

The biggest advantage of the Gree sales companies was that they were subject to Gree's management as a branch of the sales department. No promotion tricks happened between manufacturers and distributors any more. It was effective for Gree to stabilize the product's price and protect the brand image. In the operation, Dong Mingzhu strove to build a supervision system to ensure Gree's controlling power and prevent the defection of distributors. Once managers of Gree sales companies couldn't keep up with the pace or had problems in operation, Gree had the power to fire them. Gree was not the controlling shareholder in some sales companies, but still retained the authority on personnel appointment and removal.

It had been proven by many years of operating that the model of regional sales companies was the best way to confront the price wars and increasingly intensified competition. This unique sales model became a deciding factor for Gree to excel in the air conditioner market.

Gree's sales strategy was closely related to Dong Mingzhu's personal perspective. She learned that fire and water are good servants but bad masters, and in her dealings with distributors, subscribed to this mantra.

Dong Mingzhu said: "Gree's sales model was built up by Gree's team and was the result of collective wisdom. Gree's achievements can't be separated from each person's effort. As a team, we made Gree a top global brand. The essence of the Gree model was to improve and exceed itself, and keep honesty and responsibility as the eternal means to maintain vitality."

CHAPTER

5

POWERING THE BIG SHIP WITH COMBINED EFFORT

CULTIVATING A TALENTED AND LOYAL TEAM

Dong Mingzhu believed that although many factors impacted the development of an enterprise, it was the technology, management and people that were the most crucial. She believed Gree had been prepared with regard to technology and management, and now needed to focus on the cultivation of its people. It was a systematic and arduous project; no results would show in one or two days.

In Gree's evaluation systems, the first few criteria were loyalty, professionalism and caring for others. In this system, many young people had the opportunity to rise to mid-level management positions; in fact, the assistant general manager was only 31 years old. He used to be an ordinary office worker responsible for passport affairs. During the internal recruitment process, Dong Mingzhu noticed this young man had a strict and responsible work attitude, was diligent in his work and was without any complaints. When he was asked to deal with any sort of passport issues, he couldn't sleep if the issue wasn't resolved, always trying to figure out ways to fix the problem. Therefore, Dong Mingzhu earmarked him for promotion.

After more interviews and some conversations with senior staff, Dong Mingzhu was determined in her thoughts. In the discussion among senior managing staff, someone proposed assigning this young man to the human resources department, but Dong Mingzhu rejected this idea. She proposed to send him to the manufacturing plant as a factory manager. Someone raised an objection immediately, because it was a massive risk to put a 31-year-old, who had no background in technology, in the position of factory manager.

At last, Dong Mingzhu overrode all objections and assigned this young man to be the factory manager. When he started his work in the factory, he took on more work by himself, and endeavoured to solidify his understanding of technology. Meanwhile, he used his amiable characteristics to connect hundreds of factory workers with management-level staff to achieve unity in action and vision. Around seven o'clock each evening after dinner, he would go back to his office to read technology textbooks and study new products. He also spent a lot of time talking to employees to understand their positions and help them with their work.

Within a year of working in the control unit factory, he made fruitful efforts in the reorganization of factory structure, technology production and factory culture. Dong Mingzhu saw that and was very pleased. After a year, he was transferred to another department for development, after which Dong Mingzhu promoted him to be the director of the procurement department. The young man worked even harder in this new position, and reduced the cost of procurement by 20 million RMB in a year. After three years of learning on the job, Dong Mingzhu found it was the right time for him to rise to assistant general manager.

Many other young people also grew into young professionals in different positions at Gree. Gree's culture made everyone feel fulfilled in their positions. Some Gree employees appeared on the CCTV reality show Challenge Yourself. A forklift controller, Cao Xiangyun, won the championship by controlling a forklift; he could use it to open a bottle of beer or even sew!

Dong Mingzhu believed cultivating people was crucial for the sustainable development of the enterprise. It was an action that served the enterprise and employees, society and future development.

Someone asked Dong Mingzhu, "You've devoted so much to people. What if they left Gree and worked at a competitors' company? Would you regret the help you have given them?" Dong Mingzhu responded: "With regard to those who leave Gree, if they can bring Gree's culture to other enterprises, it will be a good thing."

In Gree's philosophy of personnel management, recruitment and training were indivisible, and it was Gree's duty to provide support to new employees, care about their concerns, protect their interests and contribute to a harmonious society. Besides a competitive salary and benefits in housing, pension, Medicare insurance, unemployment insurance and birth insurance, Gree provided care and support in every aspect of work and life.

CREATING A CUSTOMER BASE BY DEVELOPING A GOOD PRODUCT

Dong Mingzhu believed that whether or not an enterprise could achieve sustainable development depended on the customers' acceptance of their brand. By trial and error, she led Gree to forge a unique sales pattern that no one could imitate.

Gree achieved the highest sales revenue globally, not through price wars, but by focusing on product quality. Ensuring a quality product was Gree's winning card in the market. The focus on honesty in Gree's culture ensured that no compromise would be made regarding product quality, and codified the company's indifference to price wars, which was a display of a company's lack of confidence and a disturbance to the rate of development.

Gree's ultimate goal wasn't just to sell a product. Only if customers were satisfied with the purchase would Gree win their trust and create loyal customers. Dong Mingzhu believed it was more important to improve the product experience to the extent that no marketing of their products was needed. In the sales-oriented home appliance industry, Dong Mingzhu promoted payment before goods with a hard-line attitude and achieved an amazing result of 10 billion RMB in sales revenue at the cost of only 4 million RMB, widely considered a miracle in the industry.

For Gree's achievements in sales revenue and its independence from big chain stores, Dong Mingzhu had her own explanation: "Speaking of sales promotions, many enterprises regarded them as essential to their development. Some even deemed it as a sort of supreme weapon. It was a misunderstanding. The development of Gree stands as proof that products come before sales. Without a good product, promotions are only a pale slogan."

By 2013, Gree had been the top air conditioner vendor in China for 18 consecutive years. In addition to its powerful distribution channels, the reason for this was essentially the high quality of its products. From market responses, Gree had won the battle of credibility among customers. In the age of information, many people would research online before making a purchase, and Gree was always at the top of the recommendations. Their stellar online reputation won another large group of customers for Gree.

It had been proven that the most reliable sales figures were not built on marketing strategy, but product quality. In 1998, a newspaper needed to install 500 air conditioners and asked for a discount due to making a bulk purchase from Gree. Dong Mingzhu agreed and the purchase was made. A year later, they needed another batch and asked for an additional discount because another brand had offered a price of 500 yuan lower for each unit. This time Dong Mingzhu rejected their request, and they bought the batch from the other brand. Another year later, in 2000, the newspaper came back to Dong Mingzhu, again for a purchase of air conditioners and asked for no discount, because all the people who worked at the newspaper loved the experience they had with Gree air conditioners. These customers weren't fixated on the price; they were able to make rational choices after comparison and experience.

Gree's sales kept growing, because it met customers' needs. Gree didn't attach great importance to quality until 1993, when the problems of noise and high repair rates flared up, as with other air conditioner brands. Two different opinions regarding these issues prevailed. One party proposed that as quality improvement was a slow process, Gree needed to seize the market first and crush competitors by leveraging scale and price advantage. It should tackle the easier part first. The other party believed that product quality was the lifeline of an enterprise, and Gree needed to engage in product reform. The second party were advocates for quality reform, with Zhu Jianghong as their representative.

Dong Mingzhu always considered each issue from an overall perspective and believed that no marketing strategy would be effective without the guarantee of product quality, just as no one can build a house without a foundation. There were many reasons for an enterprise to fall apart, but most of these could be boiled down to poor product quality. Gree listened to and cared about the real needs of customers, and won more and more customers over.

ATTENTION TO DETAIL AND GOOD SERVICE THROUGH THE ENTIRE PROCESS

Dong Mingzhu realized in the beginning that the competition between different brands was made up of sales and service. Those who satisfied customer needs related to product service had the initiative in the battle. To pursue and guarantee customer satisfaction in sales and service was crucial to an enterprise's vitality and healthy development. Gree took stock and made customer satisfaction its core value, accentuated in the advertisement: 'Customer satisfaction is our eternal pursuit.'

To promote the idea of customer satisfaction, Gree's Beijing branch organized a social, promotional event. This included 'Searching for 10-Year Users of Gree', in Beijing, selected 'customer ambassadors for Gree quality', and founded the '10-year users club'. All customer ambassadors for Gree quality were invited to Gree's headquarters in Zhuhai, to visit Gree's manufacturing base and understand Gree on a deeper level.

In April 2012, Gree extended its former search for customer loyalty, 'Searching for 15-Year Users of Gree', in Heibei. Anyone who had bought Gree air conditioners before 31 July 1997 and still used them could register for the event and be given a personal ID. More than 100 people registered for the activity within five days.

In 2000 and 2011, Gree organized a 'Searching for 15-Year Users of Gree' activity in Hubei and helped qualifying customers install new inverter air conditioners for free, which Gree didn't mention in the promotion of the event, but was carried out each year. The purpose of this event was to find long-time users of Gree air conditioners and help them upgrade to new products in order to repay them for their support.

Dong Mingzhu said: "Customers' loyalty to Gree has accompanied us in this journey for more than 20 years. Gree had been trying to find loyal Gree users and repay them for their long-term support. It was also a demonstration of our product quality in hopes of winning more customers for Gree."

Of course Gree produced air conditioners primarily for profit, but Gree approached this with a focus placed firmly on high quality air conditioners rather than the money itself. Gree cared about customer service and committed to building a reputable service brand.

Gree had a unique vision for its services; that is, to extend it through the whole sales process, rather than just be focused on after-sales services. They strove to solve potential problems before customers started to use Gree air conditioners. In Dong Mingzhu's words, Gree needed to guard two gates. The first was the product quality, the second was the installation standard.

From April 1998, a blank complaint note issued by the Journal of China Association of Quality Promotion was added to the new package of Gree air conditioners, which meant it became more convenient for customers to file complaints about Gree air conditioners. It was a bold move and a confident move. No other enterprise at that time had invited this specialized publication for supervision.

In October 1999, Gree organized another influential activity, 'Feedback from 8 Million Customers', and displayed a new model of customer service. This activity lasted for more than two months. Gree mobilized more than 10,000 people to visit customers in dozens of cities and provided free air conditioner maintenance. The sold product was still Gree's business, and Gree checked on them as if visiting family members. Gree's service was welcomed by customers, and it made a positive impact on the enterprise, as well as Gree's culture.

Gree came up with the marketing slogans that 'Gree's service extends through the whole sales process', 'Gree doesn't experiment on customers', and 'High product quality saves the effort of after-sales services'. It addressed each aspect with a goal of no faults or errors in the entire product chain, from raw materials to production and transportation, and finally to installation.

So many air conditioner brands collapsed because of brutal competition over the years. Yet Gree grew and developed into the leading enterprise in the air conditioning industry and became a world champion global brand.

ABIDING BY THE RULES AND TREATING DISTRIBUTORS GENEROUSLY

Dong Mingzhu was a star in the Chinese air conditioning industry and created many innovative concepts in marketing. She led 23 sales associates to win a battle against another team with more than 1,000 people, and she took Gree to first place in sales across the nation. Because of this, some took the flight to Gree headquarters to see what kind of a woman Dong Mingzhu really was.

Dong Mingzhu believed that guaranteeing distributors' profits would benefit Gree's development in the long haul. It was a simple and practical method of business: "The profit would make distributors happy to sell your products. The goal of businesspeople was to make profit. No business-people would get involved in a non-profit business. Gree was responsible and pledged to guarantee a profit margin for distributors."

Some manufacturers only took their own interests into account and always pursued more, while overlooking the profit margin for distributors. However, Dong Mingzhu hoped for the opposite, that distributors would make more in profits than Gree. She believed this could attract and incorporate more people to Gree's business. Collectively, everyone's paddles could power this giant ship.

In 1997, Gree's distributors suffered losses at different levels in the air conditioner price war. Dong Mingzhu understood the nature of competition and decided incisively to return 250 million RMB from Gree's profits that year to distributors. Her actions resonated with distributors, and the era of Gree's market dominance dawned.

In 1996, the biggest Gree distributor, Mr An, made huge sales revenue by dumping products in certain markets, and flew to Gree headquarters to request a big discount from Dong Mingzhu, since he represented a big distributor. Dong Mingzhu immediately realized that his tricks in sales were not legitimate. The bigger his business grew, the bigger damage he would elicit for Gree. Such sales practices would have an undeniable impact on Gree's sustainable marketing and would bring immeasurable consequences. Dong Mingzhu turned him down forcefully and demanded him to sell at the settled price.

Mr An didn't reflect on his misconduct and got more aggravated, skimping on the installation fees from second-level distributors. Dong Mingzhu came to a full realization that Mr An sought nothing but profits, and sacrificed Gree's long-term profits for his immediate personal gain. Having such a person in Gree's team damaged the interests of second-level distributors and tarnished Gree's brand. Dong Mingzhu made a command immediately: to stop supplying to Mr An, which pushed him out of Gree's team.

Mr An was regretful and came to apologize to Dong Mingzhu. He also brought Zhu Jianghong as his lobbyist, but Dong Mingzhu was unswayed. Dong Mingzhu also circulated a notice to other distributors: to stop all cooperation with Mr An for a better market environment. His sales tactics disrupted the market and made business harder for everyone. Gree would lose more partners. Gree would never defend one distributor's interests at a cost to others.

Dong Mingzhu described the relationship between Gree and its distributors as "a chess game that never ends". She had her own understanding of competition and cooperation and emphasized back and forth: the one who survived in the end was the true winner. After breaking up with Gome, the specialized sales channel Dong Mingzhu had built made substantial accomplishments: it drew more than 600 distributors to join and improved Gree's market share in a very short time.

In March 2007, the relationship between Gree and Gome, the two opposing parties, underwent a subtle transition. Some experts had predicted that they would come together some day because of common interests. The nature of the business world is that it would move towards regulation, and interests would outlive friendships and hatred. Gree halted cooperation with Gome not because of faults on either side, but because of the divergence of business philosophies. As the market environment improved, Gree, as a big manufacturer, and Gome, as a big distributor, came to realize the importance of their cooperation.

In 2014, Gree upgraded its partnership with Gome and signed a deal worth 15 billion RMB, forging a strategic co-operation with Gome, who would carry a series of Gree products including air conditioners, refrigerators, water heaters and home appliances. Dong Mingzhu made a personal visit to Gome at the beginning of the year, another proof of their reconciliation.

THE ICING ON THE CAKE — LOW RETURNS AND REPAIRS

Dong Mingzhu cared deeply about Gree's brand value, but was never eager about short-term brand awareness or killing the goose that laid the golden eggs. As many air conditioner companies spared no expense on brand promotion and advertisement, Gree didn't join in the trend of publicity stunts, but built its brand image through honesty with customers, core breakthroughs in technology and consistent product quality.

Although many customers and competitors were familiar with the slogan: "Great air conditioner, Gree Brand", it didn't start out as an advertisement catchphrase, but a motto to motivate Gree employees. As time passed, it became an advertisement slogan and has remained in the public's eyes and ears all these years.

Dong Mingzhu's opinion was that advertising was an effective promotion for enterprises, but it was a flash in the pan if it was the only focus. A brand needed good products. Products of quality were the primary target for enterprises to pursue; advertisement was the icing on the cake. People at Gree buried their heads in each detail of the product, and stayed away from superfluous and impractical promotions.

In 1999, 'healthy air conditioners' became trendy. Air conditioners equipped with activated carbon, anion, medical herbs and new venting systems were launched one after another, and newly-coined words flew in the media. Many air conditioner manufacturers competed over newly added functions, and customers became confused. In 2003, during the outbreak of Severe Acute Respiratory Syndrome (SARS), the concept of healthy air conditioners boomed again. New features such as 'bacteria-proof' and 'ion-sterilization' dazzled customers in the promotions, and nearly all air conditioner brands pushed healthy air conditioners, which were considered the saviour of the industry.

Dong Mingzhu cut to the point of the matter: "The newly added functions are the result of market trends and customers needs. We shouldn't promote these new functions in such an exaggerated way. It is a publicity stunt. We shouldn't overdo the promotion."

With regard to promotion, Dong Mingzhu believed that a brand was built by products, not promotion. An enterprise should not exaggerate its products as divine, nor did it need to invest a lot in government relations or advertisements.

As long as it cared about product quality and research and development (R&D), and maintained standards in sales and services, it would naturally become competitive. The products would sell themselves. Product quality and advanced technology were the initiative for the survival and development of an enterprise. The corporate culture Dong Mingzhu promoted was different from so many other enterprises. Gree didn't build its brand as a concept, but from down-to-earth actions.

Gree would launch new products each year, a direct result of its strong R&D capacity. Dong Mingzhu believed that the development of new products was secured for the next ten years in Gree. To abate the noise of working air conditioners, Gree launched a line of 'products for sleeping time'. Gree also added ventilation to ensure the same air quality inside and outside. Considering the fact that some old people may have sore joints due to air conditioning, Gree developed auto temperature adjustment based on the detection of human body temperature. The launch of each new model from Gree would create a lot of demand in the market, which proved Dong Mingzhu's vision of high technology products and made her more resolute in Gree's efforts in R&D.

In September 2006, Gree received the honour of 'Reputable Global Chinese Brand', the first award of its kind that was conferred to an air conditioner manufacturer. In November 2006, Gree received the award of 'Chinese Quality Standard', the top award in quality evaluation. In the same month, the General Administration of Quality Supervision, Inspection and Quarantine issued the Export Exemption certificate to Gree, making it the first in the air conditioning industry to receive this honour. In November 2007, Gree was awarded 'The Most Competitive Brand' by the Ministry of Commerce. In July 2007, Gree won the honour of 'The Advanced Unit of Product Quality', issued by the Ministry of Personnel and General Administration of Quality Supervision, Inspection and Quarantine together. These top-class honours were evidence of Gree's leading position in the industry. Air conditioner distributors across the nation also proved that Gree had the lowest return and repair rates among all air conditioning brands.

CHAPTER

6

EXCELLING WITH MARKETING STRATEGIES

LEADING THE INDUSTRY TO REGULATION

In 1996, Dong Mingzhu was promoted from the director of the sales department to the general manager of Gree's Sales Company. She had a higher position and more power, but she saw the rise in power as a sign of increased responsibility. Her attitude to distributors was the same as before, she dealt with them equally and impartially. She didn't deem herself superior to the distributors or have a biased attitude towards them.

In 1996, the distributor nominated for 'Top Distributors of the Year' was unable to receive this accolade for a fourth year in a row due to a significant decrease in its revenues.

Gree always bestowed a hefty reward on its top distributors. The manager of this company felt disgraced about this loss, and asked Dong Mingzhu for help to put another company's revenue under his company's account, which could elevate his company into the top ten. He made this request not just for the reward, but also to save the honour of his company in the eyes of the industry.

Dong Mingzhu had personal connections with this company. When she was working in the Jiangsu market, she experienced strong cooperation from this company and the manager was her friend. However, she turned them down abruptly for the sake of fairness and impartiality. From her personal perspective, she hoped this company could make the top ten but, as Gree's manager, she needed to relinquish her personal favours. She believed Gree's development depended on rules and regulations. Once this kind of behaviour started, it would become hard to stop.

The manager felt terrible about this rejection, and regarded her as too cold in this matter. Dong Mingzhu didn't care about the criticism. On the contrary, she helped him to analyse the shortcomings of their strategies and advised him to expand their online sales marketing to earn new growth through earnest efforts. Her consideration didn't go in vain. This company became one of the top ten Gree distributors again in 1998.

Dong Mingzhu couldn't tolerate the misconduct of some companies seeking profits through sham publicity methods, and then not being able to honour the commitment of after-sales service. This brought a negative reputation to the whole industry. Dong Mingzhu believed that Gree couldn't achieve meaningful development alone. It needed a clean industry environment, where every player was held to regulations.

In order to change consumers' ideas about air conditioners, Dong Mingzhu engineered a situation whereby Gree would take a financial hit in order for customers to experience a higher quality product. Dong Mingzhu used the profits from high-end Gree products to balance the overall budget. Gree was not waging a price war, but rather was committed to leading the market to principled competition, where the emphasis was on the quality of the product, not low prices. From the perspective of distributors, cooperation with Gree was not a means to get rich quick, but a healthy and long-term business, which was more attractive when compared to a single deal.

While Gree was promoting an ideal sales model, it also realized the significance of a market community cultivated in the same culture and management. Dong Mingzhu told investors that Gree was always the best option for them. In this community, manufacturers and distributors pursued the same purpose of building a respected global brand. "We didn't do this for money," Dong Mingzhu said, "but we made money in the end. If you are devoted in this career, money will come as appendage."

TAKING INITIATIVE IN MARKETING WITH STRATEGY

Dong Mingzhu was a prominent figure in the Chinese household appliances industry, a businesswoman who rode the waves of the time. She innovated a new sales model of regional companies on the principle of 'the common interests of customers, business dealers and manufacturers', which was characterized by connecting investments and a dazzling array of products. This model enabled Gree to have a distribution network of more than 20,000. There were 10,000 franchised stores, 5,000 sales maintenance centres, and 30,000 maintenance specialists. Such capacity made Gree a sales champion in the air conditioning industry.

Insiders in the industry remark that Dong Mingzhu was a legendary master at sales and marketing. From 1995 onwards, she enabled Gree to secure the top place in unit sales, sales revenue and market share. By 2005, Gree took over LG and became the biggest air conditioner manufacturer and supplier in the world.

The facts had proven that Dong Mingzhu was a visionary leader and department manager. She thought in the long term and pursued sustainable interests. In other companies, sales associates were often bribed for their business, and it was the most lucrative post in a company. The situation at Gree was totally different. Dong Mingzhu thought: "The popularity of Gree's air conditioners should be credited to the front-line factory workers, and R&D engineers. The salesperson's effort only contributes a small part. It would be unreasonable for them to get the biggest benefits."

To address this, Dong Mingzhu issued a policy: Gree sales associates could not accept any payment for sales other than those that were commission earned. Even one penny would result in termination. The rule also pointed out that second-level distributors were subject to the supervision of first-level distributors. If some second-level distributors were found committing malpractice in installation or maintenance and service, the first-level distributor needed to take the responsibility and bear the consequence of their supplies being stopped.

Dong Mingzhu started her career as a sales associate. However, after she took the position of the director of the sales department, she limited the power of salespeople and cut down the number of sales groups. In the end, there were only 23 salespeople in her department. All combined, she saved tens of millions in sales expenditures, which was used to subsidize the distributors to their benefit. Dong Mingzhu led a sales team of 23 sales associates to combat rival sales teams with as many as 1,000 people. She innovated a unique sales model for Gree.

Dong Mingzhu's seemingly unreasonable reform won the support of distributors. It formed a sharp contrast with other sales models, where salespeople and distributors fought for profits, and some salespeople even left to open their own sales companies. According to the statistics, Chunlan had more than 150 salespeople in its Chongqing sales department, and the annual cost of sales and marketing was as high as 20 million RMB. Gree only had five salespeople in Chongqing, but brought in more than 300 million RMB.

To balance the business between the peak season and the low season, Dong Mingzhu initiated a strategy of 'low season rebates' in 1995, which was an effective way to bundle distributors with Gree. In the low season, Gree provided air conditioners to distributors at discount prices and distributors made bulk purchases, which solved the problem of capital deficits and overstocked inventories in the low season and alleviated the pressure to maintain a sufficient supply in the peak season. Distributors also benefitted from securing supply at a discounted price.

This sales model enabled Gree to receive 1.1 billion RMB in payment during the low season of 1995, and rebate 60 million RMB to distributors. A win-win situation was created. The strategy of off-season rebates enticed more distributors to join Gree and enlarged Gree's market.

Dong Mingzhu introduced the policy of 'year-end

rebates' immediately, in which Gree promised a certain number of rebates based on the sales of distributors by the end of the year. The bigger sales revenues distributors achieved, the bigger the rebate that was paid. It encouraged strong sales practices and developed massive distributors, who helped Gree's market expansion. The more distributors sold, the bigger the rebate they earned. A positive cycle came to fruition.

ENGAGING PARTNERS IN POSITIVE COMPETITION

Dong Mingzhu believed in a rich and profound brand culture, as well as honesty and a concern for an enterprise's character. Lack of credibility was the biggest danger for enterprises and individuals.

People who knew Dong Mingzhu were well aware that she held the established rules of the game in contempt. She always overturned them and made her own rules. She had faith in her new way, and her aggression thrust her into the spotlight of public attention.

"The market is like a chessboard," she explained. "One needs to be deliberate and meticulous in each move to gain an advantage and build an advantageous situation. To win is not to dominate the world, but to forge the future together with everyone else."

Dong Mingzhu believed in positive competition, and the principle of mutual benefits. She said, "Different parties needed to be honest and courageous, and abide by the rules of the game in cooperation. No petty tricks or attempts to take advantage of others should be allowed. The first task in positive-sum competition is to find partners who share the same ideals and business philosophies. If we are unable to reach a consensus in that respect, it will be impossible to become partners."

Dong Mingzhu was harsh and arbitrary in the consideration of distribution partnerships. Even big distributors she cultivated herself would be kicked out of Gree's team once their beliefs or actions contradicted with Gree. She required that regional distributors represent the common interests of customers, manufacturers and distributors, which was the foundation of cooperation in a positive-sum competition.

To be more accurate, the sales strategy Dong Mingzhu enforced mainly increased Gree's competitiveness in business negotiations and improved the market environment at the same time. Although many enterprises were modelling Gree's practice, the competitive environment in the air conditioning industry didn't change. Once the competition became intensified, each enterprise would play their trump card, and a price war was imminent. It would fall into the old trap of collateral damage.

Statistics show that Gree had more than 5,000 researchers and developers, two national technology centres, four research academies, 28 research centres, more than 500 laboratories, and more than 9,000 patents, of which more than 2,500 were new inventions. In 2012 and 2013, Gree's investment in R&D eclipsed 4 billion for two consecutive years, far beyond the global standard.

Many people commented that Dong Mingzhu didn't have a background in technology, and therefore didn't understand it. That was only half right. Gree filed a lawsuit on a patent for air baffles on air conditioners because another enterprise infringed on Gree's intellectual property. Reporters interviewed her on this issue, and she answered that the air baffle patent was based on practice; it was a component of Gree's patent pool, and Gree needed to guard its patent pool in the process of global expansion. She fought for every inch of land with regard to patents.

Although Dong Mingzhu was not directly involved in the process of R&D, she had a clear vision of global development trends in the air conditioning industry. She may have never considered becoming a scientist, but she appreciated the power of science. Gree's technological innovation went hand-in-hand with its sales channel reform.

From Dong Mingzhu's perspective, no one was allowed to violate the rules and regulations of the company, including herself. Everyone needed to abide by the rules and be trustworthy and resolute. Dong Mingzhu's tough characteristics left a deep imprint on Gree's culture and stimulated the overall improvement of employees.

DOING BUSINESS IN LINE WITH MORALITY

How far an enterprise can go is mainly dependent on the aspirations and ambitions of its leaders. Dong Mingzhu's vision and understanding brought huge success to Gree. She said that corporate culture was the spiritual pillar of its development; a company without it couldn't produce material or spiritual wealth, nor could it take social responsibility.

Dong Mingzhu emphasized that the growth of a business could be traced back to various factors, of which the most essential principle was to "do business in line with your morals". A successful entrepreneur must be an upright person. Most successful businesspeople and entrepreneurs had some specialized capabilities and talents. They were not only proficient in business, but also capable of being a good person. Business was their skill, and being a good person was their moral compass.

In hiring cycles at Gree, the first consideration was a person's loyalty. This requirement hinged on Dong Mingzhu's past experiences, positive or negative, in business. When Dong Mingzhu was a sales associate in Anhui, Zhu Jianghong placed the Jiangsu market in her hands. This situation made her feel uneasy; if she took the position, it would mean stealing the job from one of her co-workers. She pondered over the issue and came up with a perfect solution: to take the Nanjing market and leave the rest of the Jiangsu market to her co-workers.

Dong Mingzhu was immediately successful in the Nanjing market. Gree's sales revenue in Nanjing amounted to 36.5 million RMB within a year, 11 times that of the whole Jiangsu market in the previous year. It was the sort of miracle Dong Mingzhu often created and such achievements, of course, won her respect.

Dong Mingzhu believed that the leader of an enterprise needed vision for the industry's development and market trends, acumen for the development of products and technology, sensitivity to market potential, the ability to seize opportunities to upgrade products and claim the market with technological advantage. People were the foundation of development and the core competency of an enterprise. Enterprises needed to integrate resources, build core competency and capacity for innovation, and form an advantage in technology, brand, marketing and corporate culture.

For the benefit of the enterprise's development, Dong Mingzhu didn't cling to her glory in the 160,000 RMB Anhui market, and instead moved on to Nanjing. If she had confined herself to the Anhui market, she might still have been just a saleswoman today. She said: "Building enterprises is the reflection of your personality and morality. So is expanding the market. Gree has a common goal with its customers. As long as we build partnerships on honesty, we can create a beneficial situation."

Dong Mingzhu underlined the integration of interests from three perspectives: the interests of customers, distributors and manufacturers. She said the business principal was to combine efforts in one course so that each party would benefit from it. Actions came before interests. Enterprises needed to have the 'spirit of sacrifice'.

Dong Mingzhu believed that opportunism may induce short-term success, but the enterprise wouldn't go far this way. Gree eschewed opportunism and speculation, and pursued sustainable development. Dong Mingzhu's pursuit to be a good person and a good businesswoman prompted her to dismiss the tempting offers from other companies, and charge head on during the collective resignation incident.

Dong Mingzhu's noble view of life and values separated her from other people. She took Gree's overall development into consideration from the first day she joined, and put the company ahead of her personal interests. From the day she took the position as director of the sales department, she embarked on a new journey to lead each step of Gree's development and guide Gree to become the top air conditioner enterprise in the world. The essence of Gree's corporate culture is integrity in business.

TAKING CHALLENGES, WINNING AND VICTORY

In May 2012, the 67-year-old Zhu Jianghong announced his retirement, and a new age of Gree commenced. According to the common practice of personnel arrangement, the position of the president and the CEO wasn't to be conferred on the same person. Thus, Dong Mingzhu took the position of CEO of the Gree Group, and the former deputy director of Zhuhai's State-owned Assets Supervision and Administration Commission (SASAC), Zhou Shaoqiang, took up the post of the president and secretary of the party committee at Gree Group.

This personnel arrangement caused a ripple in the balance between the Gree Group and Gree Electric. As early as

2003, the Gree Group fell out with Gree Electric due to the issue of brand usage of Gree Electric's appliances, which resulted in Gree's former president, Xu Rong, leaving and the conviction of many former management executives.

After Zhou Shaoqiang took up the post, he naturally became a candidate to become a board member at Gree Electric, and pursued his election. Unfortunately, the plan backfired, and he lost the election at the shareholders' meeting. The post of president and CEO of Gree Electric was taken by the senior Gree employee, Dong Mingzhu.

On 25 May 2012, at the Gree shareholders' meetings, both the institutional shareholders and small shareholders directed a reverse personnel change. To an outsider's view, no doubt had been cast on the success of Zhou Shaoqiang entering the board of directors. However, he was rejected in the vote by institutional shareholders and small shareholders. According to someone in that shareholders' meeting, Zhou Shaoqiang only won about 30% of votes, so was not even close to being elected.

In the personnel arrangement, earlier announced by Zhuhai's SASAC, Gree senior employee Dong Mingzhu and SASAC personnel Zhou Shaoqiang were balanced in power, with no leaning to either side. According to another authoritative source from Gree, the new upper management had been preset before the election.

In Gree, however, Zhou Shaoqiang was no threat to Dong Mingzhu. Some shareholders expressed concern over the lack of management experience and an understanding of Gree in shareholders' meetings, and Zhu Jianghong backed up this opinion and said: "Your concern is my concern," which intensified the shareholders' distrust of Zhou Shaoqiang. They took the SASAC appointment of Dong Mingzhu as the corporate representative and CEO of the Gree Group as a sign that she would take over Gree Electric as well.

Authorities from SASAC of Zhuhai explained its personnel arrangement as a standard procedure to reorganize the structure of the management at Gree Group, especially in Gree Electric, and ensure the sustainable development of Gree.

According to the statistics bureau of Zhuhai, the annual GDP of Zhuhai was 140.323 billion RMB in 2011, while Gree's revenue was 83.517 billion RMB, accounting for two thirds of Zhuhai's overall GDP. Zhuhai reached a goal of 11% growth of GDP in 2012, which was closely related to the performance of Gree Electric. The purpose of SASAC's personnel arrangement was to ensure the balance between Gree Group and Gree Electric, and the smooth transition after Zhu Jianghong's retirement.

In the post-Zhu Jianghong era, the hope for Dong Mingzhu to be the president of Gree Electric was very high. In Gree, Dong Mingzhu and Zhu Jianghong were always neck-and-neck in management capability and personal charisma. Dong Mingzhu even outperformed Zhu Jianghong in certain aspects. Some people worried that when this balanced management ended, Gree might fall into the trap of losing voices from the technological side and the emergence of arbitrary management. These concerns were targeted at Dong Mingzhu.

However, the concerns were deemed unnecessary. On 25 May 2012, the former chairwoman of Gree Electric, Dong Mingzhu, became the chairwoman of Gree, and took up the position of president. Gree's management structure had completed a smooth transition. Starting in 1994, Dong Mingzhu had been the director of the sales department, manager of the sales company, vice general, vice chairwoman and president of Gree Electric. Now she had become the chairwoman and president of Gree Electric and president of Gree Group. A new journey had started.

DOMINATING THE MARKET WITH GOOD PRODUCTS

CONQUERING THE WORLD WITH TECHNOLOGY AND BRAND VALUE

The global household appliances market is highly competitive, especially in the air conditioning market. Gree didn't have an advantage in terms of history or capital capacity, but still came from behind to surpass their most powerful opponent, LG, within 12 years, a minor miracle that surprised the world.

Dong Mingzhu said, "Technology was the core to forging a world-class air conditioner brand. When we negotiated business with foreign clients, we didn't do it by their standard, but provided products on our own terms. Why? Because our products embodied our core technology, and we produced our own brand. We were capable of winning their respect with Gree to the same degree that we respect BMW."

It was well said by Dong Mingzhu and well performed by Gree. The company acted on those words and earned a reputation as a top global brand. Dong Mingzhu had faith in Gree in the national market and aspirations to bring Gree to the world. Gree entered the world market with its core technology and progressive beliefs, and the pride of representing the national industry and a national brand. It achieved global awareness of its products, and won the recognition and appreciation of global customers.

In September 2009, a large national media corporation published an article on Gree:

"Gree Electric Appliances Inc. of Zhuhai was founded in 1991, and is the biggest international air conditioner enterprise. It has integrated research and development, manufacturing, marketing and service. In 2008, the annual sales revenue exceeded 42.032 billion RMB, with a net profit of 1.967 billion RMB. It was listed in the Top 100 Public-listed Chinese Companies by Fortune for eight consecutive years. Since 1995, Gree had achieved the largest sales and market share in the air conditioner market for 14 years; from 2005, Gree's household air conditioner sales were the top in the world industry for four consecutive years; by 2008, Gree had acquired a global customer base as big as 88 million. As a giant manufacturer specialized in the air conditioner market, Gree strove to provide air conditioner products with advanced technology and unquestionable quality to global customers. It encompassed six manufacturing bases in Zhuhai, Chongqing, Hefei, Brazil, Pakistan and Vietnam, and had more than 40,000 employees. The annual manufacturing capacity was 27 million

in household products, and 2 million in business units. It had developed more than 20 categories, 400 series, and more than 7,000 product models to serve the needs of different customers. Gree had more than 3,000 patents, among which 300 were invention patents, the biggest in the Chinese air conditioning industry, and it is the only Chinese air conditioner enterprise independent from international technology support."

To forge a global brand, Dong Mingzhu worked in the following four dimensions: First, to build a global management system in order to improve internal organizational management and system management, build the operation capacity, accumulate international experience through internal training and external introduction, and improve international business capacity overall. Second, she wanted to build an integrated, global R&D system, to set up global R&D resource sharing and synergy through acquisition of global R&D centres and the integration of Gree R&D resources. Third, she wanted to build a global supply chain system to make use of Gree's advantages in speed, efficiency and cost control and build a comprehensive system of procurement, manufacture and logistics to further improve efficiency and cost-effectiveness. Finally, she wanted to develop high-end products to improve the technological value and brand value, and create a brand image by improving product design and core technology.

Dong Mingzhu pointed out that globalization was just the start for Gree in its endeavour to build and maintain sustainable competitiveness, and produce first-class product and brand value. In her mind, a good marketing strategy wasn't limited to making profits by selling products, but included the pursuit of common interests in the partnership between manufacturers and distributors. Gree protected customers' interests and partnerships with distributors, and maintained a product standard, which made Gree's business more substantial in long-term development and international expansion.

ENHANCING THE FOUNDATION

Dong Mingzhu appreciated the philosophy of Lao Tzu, that "great undertakings have small beginnings, and difficult tasks are tackled from where it's easiest". She believed that attention to detail was the reflection of a serious and scientific attitude. To pursue an excellent product at any cost was essential to Gree's brand, while marketing was just a plus. Gree needed to concentrate on the development of good products and avoid exaggerated marketing to build a brand image.

From the start of the new century, Dong Mingzhu had been contemplating new ways to preserve Gree's advantage in competition. Society had entered into the era of the service economy, and customer service was spotlighted in marketing activities. There was no doubt that good service quality was the prevalent weapon in competition, and essential for the survival of a business. Customer service was the after-sales service, which mostly boiled down to maintenance, in many people's opinion. However, Gree had different philosophies and approaches to this.

As a prominent figure in the air conditioning industry, Dong Mingzhu had her own understanding and interpretation of after-sales service: the products that needed no extra servicing were quality products, and enterprises that needed no after-sales servicing were good enterprises. Gree's philosophy was simple: even a small concern for a customer was a big matter to Gree. By working with this philosophy, Gree regulated itself in the manufacturing process and kept itself responsible to customers. After-sales service was a distraction and burden to customers. When they bought the product, they didn't do it to use after-sales services. Many people believed that good after-sales service put customers at ease, but a product that guaranteed no need of extra servicing would truly satisfy customers, which was even better.

A saying that "a good customer experience depended 30% on product quality and 70% on installation" prevailed in the Chinese air conditioning industry. Without an installation service, no customers would purchase air conditioners, and no sales would happen. Dong Mingzhu believed if Gree air conditioners were installed properly, the product would need no after-sales service. In the few cases of after-sales services requests at Gree, 80% were caused by improper installation by distributors. Thus, Gree included installation fees into the manufacturing cost, and paid distributors or maintenance centres to provide free installations to customers to guarantee the quality of the installation. Dong Mingzhu allowed no failures at any juncture.

Every year, Gree devoted a lot of human resources and expenditure to installation training in each maintenance and service centre, and reinforced the supervision of installation quality, as well as rewards and punishments.

The servicing of air conditioners was a big headache for customers; therefore, Gree improved service networks to protect their customers. All Gree after-sales services were provided by their sales company, which ensured customers' rights and a secured profit margin for manufacturers and distributors. Gree built more than 5,000 service centres across the nation, and trained more than 30,000 maintenance staff to serve in those locations. Gree also launched a series of new initiatives, such as presenting the Household Air Conditioner Installation Training Certificate and the Gree Air Conditioner Installation Training Certificate to installation personnel. They also built up a team of 'first responders' and 'Gree experts in after-sales service', which together upgraded Gree's services and ensured a quick response to customers' needs. Gree adhered to the principle 'Customers' interests first, Gree's second'. Dong Mingzhu emphasized on different occasions that only when customers were satisfied with the purchases, could Gree earn its profits.

On 1 January 2005, Gree implemented a new service policy in air conditioners, giving a free six-year warranty, even though the national requirements were a one-year warranty of the unit and three years for the components, surpassing the national standard by a large degree. The working duration for air conditioners was eight to ten years on average. Gree's six-year warranty almost covered the whole duration, equivalent to a lifetime warranty. This standard exceeded all other domestic brands, and made Gree a leader in global standards.

FULFILLING PROMISES AND ADDRESSING CUSTOMER CONCERNS

Gree had a famous slogan that even a small concern for customers was a big matter for Gree. It took care of customers' concerns and won customers' respect. Actions spoke louder than words.

Dong Mingzhu said we should never deceive customers with alluring promises, but educate them with actions. She believed that it is an enterprise's responsibility to guide customers to choose safe yet affordable brands, and realize the value of their purchase.

Dong Mingzhu pointed out that to strike a win-win situation required an enterprise to have honesty and commitment to their promises. Honesty is the foundation of partnerships and a lack of credibility has led entire enterprises into ruin. Some of them had exaggerated or blatantly lied about new features to sway the public towards their product. For example, they boasted how their engines were built by global companies or how they used advanced foreign technology, which was irresponsible and dishonest.

Gree's commitment to a six-year warranty for the unit was a manifestation of its confidence in its products. This commitment was not only a promise to customers, but a demand Gree placed on itself. Dong Mingzhu said that the failure to fulfil a promise was dishonest and would cost customers ultimately. This motivated the company to make outstanding products and this promise was a catalyst to improve product quality, which in turn reduced after-sales service. Almost no maintenance was called in for six years, which benefited customers and Gree's profits as well.

Some enterprises eschewed competition, but Gree, led by Dong Mingzhu, was not one of them. She had faith in Gree's product quality and technology. The bid for the air conditioners to be installed in the Olympic Media Village in 2008 attracted brands with the most advanced technology. Gree emerged as the best among the bids from domestic and international brands, and became the authorized air conditioner supplier of the Olympic Media Village. Its trump card was that Gree air conditioners would kick in automatically, even in bitterly cold temperatures below -25°C, a unique selling point of Gree's range. Gree's innovative technology had helped them win the bid.

More than 5,000 Gree air conditioners were installed in the Olympic Media Village, where global media gathered.

The installations received good feedback, which could be attributed to the foundation of advanced technology on which Gree's products were built.

In Dong Mingzhu's marketing philosophy, product quality and whole-process service outweighed advertisements and Gree didn't create many promotional concepts. Dong Mingzhu said: "Advertisements can't make a global brand. The core of success is advanced technology. Gree possessed more than 9,000 technology patents, of which 2,500 were original inventions. From household units to business units, all are produced with our own technology. Our core technology has been applied to products in the first five-star hotel in Huangshan, which is just one example. I believe Gree could achieve things beyond our imagination. We won't be satisfied with our achievements, but will keep pushing ourselves towards excellence, to keep the leading position in the world. "

In 2009, Gree achieved the highest sales revenue in the world in the category of household appliances, according to the China World Records Association, and broke many records in China as well as the world. Gree has continued to produce the best-quality air conditioners and has endeavoured in every aspect, from the selection of companies to produce their components, to unlimited R&D investment, which laid the foundation for its leading position in the world air conditioning industry. The sales revenue of Gree household air conditioners has ranked first in China for 18 consecutive years, starting in 1995, and has ranked first in the world for eight consecutive years, since 2005.

The commitment to their promise and 'zero concerns for customers' has built the stellar service standard of

Gree, and the company has continued to innovate new products and business models to maintain its leading position in the world.

MAKING A SACRIFICE AND PROMOTING THE INDUSTRIAL SPIRIT

Dong Mingzhu advocated an 'industrial spirit' among Chinese enterprises. She thought it was different from business entrepreneurship, as industrial development was built brick by brick. The foundation decided how high it could go; chance and speculation didn't work. Only meticulous work could help achieve it, step by step. Dong Mingzhu used her experiences to illustrate that the transition from business entrepreneurship to industrial spirit was the core objective of Chinese enterprises.

In Dong Mingzhu's interpretation, the industrial spirit was less empty talk and more practical work, catering to customer' needs, taking social responsibility, leading social development, and being responsible to the future, which was also known as 'the spirit of sacrifice'.

"In my mind," she said, "the real industrialists are practitioners of an 'industrial spirit', who have ideals, ambitions, visions and a sense of social responsibility. True industrialists take it as their main objective to promote social progress, rather than just make a profit. The development of China hinges on these real industrialists and the industrial spirit. Profit is not their only purpose, but the appendage of technological innovation and development. I don't regard myself as a smart person, but I am determined in my direction, and that is Gree Electric. I hope it develops into a global brand, the pride of our nation in the air conditioning industry. To achieve this goal, we only make air conditioners, have built the biggest air conditioner laboratory in China and serve our customers wholeheartedly."

Dong Mingzhu believed that true success would be hard to make without some sacrifice. She started as a sales associate, and grew to be the president and CEO of Gree Electric, with her youth and effort devoted to Gree's business. She was upset by the clamorous society where money was the ultimate goal of business development, and the renunciation of social responsibility. Even some local governments overlooked balanced development and were caught up in profit-seeking.

Dong MIngzhu believed that all businesspeople and industrialists pursue profits, but with different approaches. Industrial spirit was closely related to science and technology, and an extension of science and technology. Compared to business practices, credibility, equal competition and long-term value were emphasized more by an industrial spirit. Dong Mingzhu's persistence prompted Gree's breakneck development and attracted more insightful personnel to join the group.

Dong Mingzhu tried to emphasize that the pursuit of business profits created slack teams, because they cut corners and resorted to extreme measures to make profits and neglected the R&D of products. It became a habit. The effort to make lucrative profits in the short term would cause the technology to fall behind.

Dong Mingzhu's life goal was to build Gree into a reputable global brand and a figure of national pride. Dong Mingzhu was persistent in her belief: to be a responsible person, to take on challenges and build a responsible enterprise to serve the nation and wider society. In 2013, she had made Gree a reputable enterprise with an annual sales revenue of 120 billion RMB. Gree was the leader in global air conditioner sales in 2005, a seemingly impossible feat in the household appliances industry in China. With her industrious spirit, she focused on developing a made-in-China brand, broke world records, and won praise from the world: "Good products, made in China!"

GOOD PRODUCTS ARE THE BEST MARKETING STRATEGY

Dong Mingzhu, when thinking back to Gree's battle with Gome, explained: "Some people thought our confrontation with Gome was because of Gree's capacity. Others felt as though Gree gave Gome a black eye, because they didn't dare to challenge Gome themselves. Some thought Gree was to blame, but I don't think so. Gome asked brands to abide by their standards, and we were capable of saying no to that. I knew our capacity. Gree was considered a reputable brand among customers. That was our base."

She also pointed out that the key for the sustainable development of an enterprise was to answer customer' needs and produce good products. And good products would win customers' trust and build a good reputation, and we would have the market: "If customers wanted to buy our products, they wouldn't care who they bought it from. Our market was secure because of customers, not because of stores of distributors. We wouldn't sell at your store if we disagreed with your requirements; we had our principles. We would end a partnership if a company's requirements were in conflict with our principles. We sincerely hoped to come to a consensus with big distributors such as Gome. We were not pursuing a self-distributing channel or using it as a tool to confront big chain stores. We were looking for partners with the same ideals, and sustained Gree's development together."

Dong Mingzhu realized earlier that most discounts in the air conditioner market were the consequence of competitive price wars with other brands. Ferocious battles in the air conditioner market were detrimental to the industry. On one hand, the price war scaled down profit margins, and the enterprises suffered as a consequence of deficient reinvestment. This challenged the development of the enterprise and curtailed tax earnings for the country. On the other hand, the price cuts propelled enterprises to recalculate the costs of manufacturing and services, which, in turn, harmed the interests of customers and induced the pitfalls of a market where ultimately nobody gains.

Dong Mingzhu thought that the diminutive profits earned in the air conditioning industry was an unwavering development trend. Because Gree had built its own brand, it still controlled the profit margin and insisted on not increasing the price. Gree had the strong foundations to survive and develop, and bring better service to customers. First, Gree kept innovating new models and provided cost-effective products with improvements in efficiency. Second, the advantage of scale manufacturing equalled out the increase in raw materials required by other sectors.

What was more remarkable was that Gree still shunned diversification, even with the tiny profits available in the air conditioning industry. Dong Mingzhu believed that if Gree couldn't produce high quality air conditioners, how could it excel in other fields? As early as 1997, the temptation of diversification loomed large on Gree's horizon. Some manufacturers not in the air conditioner market offered their enterprises for acquisition and merger. Gree weighed up the advantages and disadvantages and rejected these offers. Gree persisted on the road to specialization, to make high quality air conditioners, perfect in function and service to the customer.

Dong Mingzhu emphasized there are national and global standards for products, but the highest standard came from customers. Customer satisfaction was the highest standard Gree wanted to pursue. "Personally, I believed in a broad vision," Dong Mingzhu said. "The consideration of national will, which helped to combine the enterprises' interests with national interests, which was to serve the people, and generated more actions beneficial to people and society. That was our direction. Gree was a global brand now. We couldn't only focus on the local influence. We shouldered the national image."

Gree's sales revenue in 2013 reached 118.6 billion RMB, with a year-on-year increase of 19.44%. Dong Mingzhu proposed a goal for 2014 to expand revenue to 140 billion

RMB, which was 8 billion more than the previous goal of increasing by 20 billion RMB every year.

CHAPTER

MANAGING WITH AN WITH AN IRON FIST AND HIGH MORALS

DOMINEERING TO ENFORCE REGULATIONS

Dong Mingzhu was known for her domineering attitude and iron-fisted actions in business management. She held the same standard for her employees and always said, "You could also accomplish what I have."

Those two characteristics manifested in her management. She believed that a big mistake should be tolerated, but a small one needed to be punished, because no one would be committed to making big mistakes and destroying their reputation, but some small mistakes were deliberate. For instance, some employees would push their luck by not being punctual, and it couldn't be tolerated. They may have thought, "I just made a small mistake. What can you do to me?" Hence, Dong Mingzhu tolerated big mistakes and punished small ones.

When she was promoted to be the director of the sales department, she was faced with a big mess. No regulations were in place. Employees read newspapers or talked to each other during work. No professionalism was cultivated. She knew any large reform might infringe on the interests of some higher-management leaders, and Dong Mingzhu would become the target for all and suffer the consequences.

From the first day of work, Dong Mingzhu didn't like the slack atmosphere in the sales department, where people held a cup of tea or a newspaper and talked all day long. She initiated a weekly meeting where she spent almost half a day emphasizing discipline and criticized the individuals who didn't adhere to it. Some were reduced to tears on the spot. Most employees were females from the sales department. Dong Mingzhu issued clear instructions on dress code and behavioural standards. She asked everyone to cut their hair short or wear a hair bun during work and no flashy accessories were allowed during work time.

Dong Mingzhu's determination in reforming the enforcement of discipline was a tool to serve her purpose. From her perspective, the livelihood of employees depended on enterprises, either in a state-owned or joint-stock system. If Gree fell apart, the first group to bear the consequences would be her employees. If she only considered her personal interests, it was unnecessary to become adversarial with anyone. Dong Mingzhu didn't pursue frivolous things. She would get tp the heart of the matter for the development of Gree, even at the risk of displeasing someone.

Dong Mingzhu's reforms continued. Some couldn't stand it and became intent on overturning her. They started to hurl abuse at her in letters to higher management. Dong Mingzhu turned a blind eye to them. She believed facts spoke for themselves, and fabricated rumours wouldn't stand. She believed as long as she fought for the company's interests, she would have no vulnerability for them to attack.

Dong Mingzhu always said: "Harmony is achieved through fighting!" Her strictness applied to each employee in the sales department and all of Gree. In 2001, Gree's sales revenue hit 10 billion RMB for the first time, and everyone was overjoyed. However, some people in charge of procurement and finance acted illegally, following implicit rules and stealing company possessions. Dong Mingzhu tackled this seriously and sent one finance manager to prison through the legal process.

Some people said Dong Mingzhu projected her own pursuits onto other people. It made sense in a way. Each person had different ambitions. In the eyes of an aggressive person, a man idle all day long must have no ambition, and this kind of person was not suitable to work under Dong Mingzhu's style. The development of an enterprise needed a domineering character like Dong Mingzhu to steer the direction. Dong Mingzhu limited the relative freedom of employees, but built the force of the sales department.

Being selfless and fearless, and speaking through her actions, Dong Mingzhu inspired Gree employees with actions and experiences: "If we are not responsible, just working for a salary and caring about short-term interests, when our enterprise doesn't make any profit, it will be a bad day for us."

CONCENTRATING ON TESTS BEFORE PRODUCT LAUNCH

Though hailed as a marketing genius, Dong Mingzhu proposed that: "Good marketing will never be enough; product quality is the priority." In a broad sense, marketing emphasized products as well. Dong Mingzhu said this to emphasize product quality, which was the reason customers made their purchases. Only the products with trustworthy quality could sell well, support the manufacturers dealing with distributors, and sell through customers' reviews rather than high-cost advertisements.

Gree adhered to the principle to "never test underdeveloped products on customers", and didn't launch any immature products to the market. The R&D team would repeatedly run tests on independently developed products and unravel all potential problems before they could enter the market. In the process of developing new products, Gree would consider things from the customers' perspectives, meticulously analyse the market, and strive to serve customer' needs to the greatest extent. Newly designed products needed to go through the trial manufacturing process, trial working tests, adjustments, and all kinds of evaluations before they were manufactured and launched in the market.

When all other brands launched inverter air conditioners to seize the market, Gree did the opposite. It postponed the launch of its 'Silent King' series and concentrated on the further study of their products. Gree scrutinized each wind blade to increase air volume passage and reduce noise. Gree strove to develop technology that would produce a higher degree of refrigeration at the same power output used by others in the industry, even if only by 0.1% in efficiency.

According to national standards, the temperature of the capacitance for household appliances needed to maintain 600 working hours at 70°C. Gree outdid the standard and considered 1,000 working hours in the same condition as suitable for qualified products. For copper pipe and other auxiliary materials, Gree purchased from the biggest international providers, whose products were the best in quality, and the price was 5% higher than others. After a series of quality control tests and evaluations, Gree launched the "Silent King" series and made a hit in the market.

Starting in 1995, Gree started a comprehensive quality rectification project and launched '12 regulations of the general manager', which was later developed into '14 regulations of the president', and regulated each operation that was prone to malpractice with extreme consequences. Any employees who violated one of the regulations would be fired with no other consideration. These tough measures pushed the improvement of Gree's quality.

To ensure quality standards, the technology department, quality control department, business management department and assembly factory shared responsibility. Zhu Jianghong, the general manager at that time, asked someone to put a big hammer in the assembling factory. If any air conditioners fell short of the standards, managers from the four departments would smash them in front of all the factory workers and punished those who were responsible.

Dong Mingzhu believed that Gree needed to endeavour both in product quality and marketing, and attached equal importance to both. Even the greatest marketing strategy couldn't sell a bunch of invaluable products, and the best products couldn't stand out without proper marketing. Any loose link in manufacturing or marketing would impede the development of enterprises. From this perspective, Dong Mingzhu spared no effort on the emphasis of product quality.

Gree never tested underdeveloped products on customers, which won Gree the electric market, as well as trust and accolades from customers and the media. The reason for Gree's popularity among customers could be boiled down to desirable products. The advertisement slogan "Great air conditioner, made by Gree" endowed Gree with the concept of good quality. When customers saw Gree air conditioners, they recognized dependable quality. Dong Mingzhu said: "The goal of Gree is to build a brand that everyone trusts, like they trust the brand BMW."

UNYIELDING TO DISREPUTABLE PRACTICES AND FIGHTING FOR HARMONY

Dong Mingzhu believed in the philosophy of fighting in the business world, and, as previously mentioned, that "harmony was struck by fighting". This was not because of her nature. She just believed a fighting spirit was crucial in business management. In Gree's headquarters in Zhuhai, Dong Mingzhu fought contemptible practices all the time.

In 2001, the 47-year-old Dong Mingzhu took the position of general manager of Gree Electric. Gree was the largest enterprise in the Zhuhai special economic zone, with more than 6,000 employees. As the general manager of the largest Chinese air conditioning enterprise, Dong Mingzhu was supposed to direct all her effort to business operations during the prime sales season. She hadn't expected to be involved in any incidents of 'inner strife'.

From May 2011, media across the nation reported on "the internal strife of Huaidi" with sensational titles like "The Surprising Internal Conflict in Gree – the Suspension in Gree May Spread Nationwide", "The Inside Secrets of Gree's Internal Strife at Huaidi", "The Internal Conflict in Gree – What's Sister Dong's Move in this Situation?" or more subtle headlines like "Gree Ran into Big Problems in its Traditional Advantage of Distribution Channel". Some articles posed the question with sarcasm: "How will Dong Mingzhu deal with this imminent danger in her ultimate strategy?"

The 'internal strife in Gree' was provoked by a personnel dismissal. Senior executive Liang Jun in Gree Electric at Huaidi was involved in marketing practices that damaged Gree's overall development. To protect the interests' of customers and distributors, he was dismissed from his post.

The Huaidi Gree sales company was built in the autumn of 1999 as one of the first few Gree sales companies. Gree's market in Huaidi was controlled by five big distributors. Gree air conditioners were circulated from Huainan to Huaibei (cities in Anhui Province) at their discretion, which endangered the profits of principled Gree distributors.

This appalled Dong Mingzhu. Customers wanted to purchase the product at a lower price. If some cheaper Gree products were prevalent in the market, people would stop buying the higher-priced products, and even wait for a long time for the cheaper product to restock. In this way, the 100,000 yuan's worth of cheaper products, which were circulated from outside the region, would keep the higher quality products, worth 10 million RMB, locked in a warehouse. Small local distributors would suffer a loss or even bankruptcy. Dong Mingzhu dismissed Liang Jun. Then the infighting at Gree's sales company in Huaidi broke out.

The incident in Huaidi was complicated. Dong Mingzhu handled dissenting executives from Huaidi, who went to great lengths to bring her down. They spread false news about Dong Mingzhu and Gree in news conferences and slandered Dong Mingzhu at public events and sent threatening letters to her. Dong Mingzhu weathered the storm and steadfastly cleaned up the sales company at Huaidi. The market was restored to order.

Since Dong Mingzhu had started to work in the headquarters, she was involved in all kinds of fights and games to protect the development and integrity of Gree. She waged wars against dishonest distributors and undisciplined colleagues with higher connections, deputy managers who abused their power, or even members of her own family, whose conduct may have endangered Gree's development. Her unyielding nature in the fights made others think that, "no grass would grow on the land she stepped on", but that was just a comment from her opposition.

Dong Mingzhu became even stronger through trials and tribulations. She got to the root of the problem, drove Gree out of the stagnant trap, and led to scientific and regulated management. As a lot of other air conditioning enterprises went through bankruptcy, Gree, which didn't have the advantage originally, became even stronger and grew into a leading business worldwide.

TEAMING UP AND WINNING OVER THE GREE BRAND

The thriving prospects of Gree proved that a state-owned company was as vigorous as a private-owned one, as long as effective management was in place. Gree was confident about the competition and challenges, but a fierce battle for the usage of Gree's brand broke out. The president, Zhu Jianghong, and general manager, Dong Mingzhu, of Gree Electric waged this war for a new chapter of Gree's development.

On 28 October 2003, an article was published on *Guangdong-Hong Kong Information Daily*: "Gree Marched into Kitchen Appliances Market". The Chinese finance information website also reported in the title that Gree had built three household appliances bases and that Gree had entered the kitchen appliances market and predicted 1.5 billion in manufacturing capacity in five years. These articles were for the promotion of Gree household appliances.

A week later, on 4 November, Gree Electric made a serious announcement that these articles, as published in the newspaper or website, hadn't verified the facts with Gree. The reports were fabricated, with no foundation in facts, and seriously misled consumers. The announcement also explained that as a publicly listed company, Gree was the biggest air conditioner manufacturer and only produced air conditioners, not any other household appliances. The brand name Gree was used exclusively on air conditioner products. Any other usage or promotion based on Gree Electric or Gree air conditioners was illegal.

The infringement of Gree's brand, indicated in the announcement, was conducted by Gree Household Appliances, which belonged to Gree Group and was called Gree Household Electric Appliances, Zhuhai at that time. Zhu Jianghong and Dong Mingzhu's announcement took Gree Group by surprise. The infighting over the usage of Gree's brand evolved into a war between the company and its controlling shareholders. Some media outlets described it as a "war between father and son".

Gree Electric belonged to the state-owned Gree Group in terms of assets. The Gree Group, previously known as Zhuhai Economic Development General Corporation, was established in 1985 with the authorization of the Zhuhai government. As a state-owned corporation, it carried the mission of protecting and increasing the value of state-owned assets. In 2003, the gross annual output of Gree

Group was 15.1 billion RMB, accounting for one seventh of the industrial output of Zhuhai. Gree Group owned the industrial manufacturers as their main business and developed in the trade and real estate fields as well. It owned famous brands like Gree and Rossini.

For Gree Electric, the brand Gree was the intangible asset of the enterprise. The trademark was created by Gree Electric in 1991. Back then, Gree was not a public company. It was a subsidiary of Gree Group and had no choice but to let Gree Group use its brand. Due to its small influence at that time, no other subsidiary companies would use its brand. However, as it became more prominent, other subsidiary companies fought to use the brand name Gree, or even Gree Electric.

If all the household appliances products of the Gree Group used the brand, it would mislead customers. Hence, Zhu Jianghong and Dong Mingzhu waged a prolonged and arduous battle with Gree Group. It turned out to be what Zhu Jianghong and Dong Mingzhu expected. In September 2004, Gree Electric acquired four other subsidiary companies worth 148 million RMB, namely Lingda Compressor Company, Gree Household Electric Appliances, Gree Wire, and Xinyuan Electronics. On 21 December 2005, Gree Group and Gree Electric signed a transfer agreement of the brand name Gree, and Gree Electric acquired exclusive usage of the Gree brand.

The day of 27 March 2006 was worth celebrating for both Zhu Jianghong and Dong Mingzhu, because the transfer of the brand of Gree had finally been completed. The state trademark office approved the application for transferring Gree's brand trademark to Gree Electric, and it took

immediate effect. The three-year fight over the brand between Gree Group and Gree Electric came to an end. Zhu
Jianghong and Dong Mingzhu had both won this battle.

CLEANING THE HOUSE AND DISPELLING THE CLOUDS

Dong Mingzhu always worried about the market when she was involved in different kinds of internal conflicts. Between 2003 and 2005, the restructuring of Gree Electric was the biggest disturbance in her professional life. Gree Electric's prospects were unclear, with the Zhuhai municipal government and external investors involved.

Since 2004, the Gree Group had changed its senior personnel regularly. A vice-president of the Gree Group and a few managers from Gree's real estate market and Lingda Compressor Company were also detained or imprisoned. As many high-level executives were arrested, a black hole in the Gree Group was exposed. This felt ominous and Dong Mingzhu was worried: "This permissive attitude has caused the loss of tens of millions in state-owned assets. Were there not some hidden secrets behind this? "

Dong Mingzhu thought that the restructuring of state-owned enterprises came down to personnel arrangement. People could make anything happen and good people made excellent enterprises. It was so simple. As long as the right people were in place, the state-owned system would eliminate problems. Some people didn't work hard because the company was state-owned. If Gree Electric followed this path, it couldn't be successful. To work in a state-owned company you needed to resist temptation and maintain a spirit of sacrifice.

RESTRUCTURING PROCESS

In Dong Mingzhu's opinion, the restructuring process needed to safeguard state-owned assets and maintain the sustainable development of the enterprise. As long as state-owned assets were not devalued, the approaches could be flexible. Gree Electric was a good example of this. It used to have a deficit of 50 million RMB on its account, but had now stockpiled 2 billion RMB. This was due to the appreciation of its assets. The state could get their investment back, and the enterprise could achieve sustainable development. This was the best way of restructuring.

This restructuring storm brought a lot of trouble to Zhu

Jianghong, who was the president of Gree Electric at that time. In December 2003, *Guangdong-Hong Kong Information Daily* published an article under the title "Another Chu Shijian Appeared in Gree", implicating Zhu Jianghong as another Chu Shijian, the former president of Yunnan Hongta Group. It is said that Zhu Jianghong tried to claim 30% of the company shares out of the 58%, which was owned by Gree Group through equity replacement and MBO restructuring. The article classified Zhu Jianghong as the "59-year-old phenomenon" who was going to encroach on state-owned assets before retirement.

This was defamation. In 2004, Zhu Jianghong filed a lawsuit against the writer Zhong Dajun, who had tarnished his reputation. Zhu Jianghong won the court ruling. Zhong Dajun was asked to apologize in the newspaper and provide 100,000 RMB compensation for the trauma.

Meanwhile, rumours about strange account activity, the establishment of a small treasury, and the cooking of account books in Gree circulated. The Zhuhai Discipline Inspection Commission and Industrial and Commercial Bureau sent staff for investigation. Some people from Gree Group had a clear goal: to kick Zhu Jianghong and Dong Mingzhu out of Gree.

In the battle between Gree Electric and Gree Group, Gree Group tried hard to win Dong Mingzhu over. They sent someone to negotiate with Zhu Jianghong and Dong Mingzhu, and offered Zhu Jianghong a yearly salary of two million for five years if he retired now and offered Dong Mingzhu the choice of the position of president or chairwoman in Gree Group. If they didn't accept that, they would call in a shareholders' meeting to dismiss Zhu Jianghong.

Zhu Jianghong laughed at their offer and said: "I wouldn't and couldn't take your money. This is illegal." He didn't care about the position of chairman of the board. If he resigned, it was not his loss, but the loss of the enterprise and the government.

This critical period inspired a fighting spirit and capacity in Dong Mingzhu. She told Zhu Jianghong that this was not a matter of personal choice. Gree Group had lost billions of RMB. If they took over Gree Electric, it would soon follow suit. The state-owned assets were endangered.

On 23 May, before the former chairman Xu Rong could go to the shareholders' meeting and dismiss Zhu Jianghong from the position of chairman of Gree Electric, he received a notice from the Zhuhai municipal government, which banned him from the meeting. This battle ended with Xu Rong's resignation in January 2004.

The Zhu Dong Team had won the final game. The cloud was dispelled. Gree Electric was still shining in Zhuhai, like a rainbow after the storm.

CHAPTER

9

INNOVATING INDEPENDENTLY AND LEADING THE TRENDS

PROPOSING SUPPORT FROM THE GOVERNMENT

Dong Mingzhu had advocated to government for the support of local enterprises and the end of inclination towards international brands.

As the representative for NPC and Chinese People's Political Conservative Conference sessions, in 2007 Dong Mingzhu proposed that the policy of government procurement should be inclined to innovative national enterprises. Dong Mingzhu said: "As a matter of fact, many national enterprises have surpassed international corporations in terms of technology and are fully qualified to meet government procurement standards, but some local governments have issued the notice that 'only foreign brands will be considered' in some bidding processes, and have shunned national brands. From my perspective, as long as the product quality of a national brand is in the same line as foreign ones, or better than them, the government should support the national enterprises unconditionally."

Although the Chinese government had placed more emphasis on innovation, and enterprises were striving in that direction by promoting their technology to adhere to advanced global standards, Dong Mingzhu was upset with the issue that only foreign brands would be considered in the government procurement process.

On 25 November 2006, the Hefei government issued the Notice for Placing Bids on the Central Air Conditioning System in the Compound of Municipal Bureau of Land and Resources. The Hefei Government Affairs Development Investment Corporation would preside over the bidding. The notice specified that the bid also included two sets of screw chillers and cooling towers, and several centrifugal pumps and terminal equipment; the bid for the sets of screw chillers and centrifugal pumps was only open to original products from Europe and America.

The specified notice rendered Gree unqualified for the bid, despite its leading position in the domestic and international air conditioner markets. Even though Gree excelled in its product quality and technology, its 'birth place' was not in line with the requirements, and it lost the bid before it was started. The government administration didn't contribute its share of responsibility in the development of national enterprises and acted exactly to the contrary. No wonder people were bewildered and upset.

Each government level gave great importance to Dong Mingzhu's suggestion. In 2008, Zhuhai initiated the plan for the "Evaluation Process of Government Procurement on Innovated Products", which supported innovative national enterprises on the level of policy and secured the advantages of local innovative enterprises in the competition for government procurement.

Gree air conditioners were representative of an innovative, energy-efficient and environment-friendly national brand in Zhuhai, and the Zhuhai government implemented Gree's policy in a massive procurement project. Gree was selected to be the contract supplier for government procurement and was the prioritized or designated product in some projects. Gree basically took over the government procurement market. In 2008 and 2009, Gree's air conditioners accounted for 97% and 98%, respectively, of all air conditioner purchases in Zhuhai.

In June 2009, Guangdong Province also introduced "Suggestions on Government Procurement of Innovative Products Developed in Guangdong", an earmarked pathway of innovative national brands in government procurement projects. Dong Mingzhu said these policies prompted huge momentum in innovation. She also proposed that special policies should be designed for start-up businesses that were disadvantaged in competition because of their scale. The government should grant special consideration to small- and medium-sized enterprises (SMEs) in procurement, lower the threshold for entrance to the bidding process, and develop complementary mechanisms between large enterprises, as well as SMEs.

In 2011, the Ministry of Finance and the Ministry of Industry and Information Technology issued "Interim Measures to Promote the Development of Small- and Medium-Sized Enterprises through Government Procurement", which set forth 18 regulations and came into effect on 1 January 2012. It demanded no restrictions on the entrance into the government procurement bidding process for SMEs, and no discrimination on small- and middle-sized governments on the grounds of registered capital, general assets, annual revenue, employees size, annual profits or tax paying.

All these measures provided a support platform for national enterprises in the act of government procurement. Dong Mingzhu was gratified.

ESTABLISHING GREE STORES FOR BRAND EXPANSION

After ten years of operation, Dong Mingzhu believed that the sales channel of Gree was healthy. More than 10,000 globally scattered Gree Stores served the undeniable function of improving market shares.

In March 2006, two giant chain stores, Gome and Suning, announced a procurement plan for air conditioners in the new year worth a few billion RMB all together. Gome announced five billion in contracts for mainstream air conditioner brands, which could reach 40% of the market in 2006. Almost all national and global air conditioner brands showed up to Gome's procurement event.

Unexpectedly, Gree's president, Dong Mingzhu, didn't show up, another cold shoulder turned to Gome. Gome had sent invitations for the event to Gree and clearly desired Gree's participation.

Dong Mingzhu turned down Gome's invitation in line with her original beliefs. All she pursued was autonomy in price setting for Gree. She could sell air conditioners at a reasonable price in Gree Stores to earn more market shares instead of depending on Gome.

Some people were worried that Gree's market share would suffer a recession after it turned down Gome, and it would have to seek cooperation in distribution channels after its own channel lost its efficiency. However, Gree opened one store after another with great momentum. People started to understand that Gree had confidence in its own stores, and its uncooperative decision was not a rash act.

Dong Mingzhu believed that different brands suited different distribution channels. High-end products were always sold in their own store, while ordinary products were sold in department stores or chain stores. It was the common international practice.

Dong Mingzhu believed in Gree's model because she had realized the disadvantages of chain store channels long ago. After Gree's conflict with Gome during the price war, Dong Mingzhu was more inclined to build up Gree's own channels. The success of trial stores gave her confidence in the belief that the Gree Store was a better sales model and would contribute heavily to Gree's development.

Manufacturers in China had a love-hate relationship with department stores or chain store channels, which were the main sales channels and responsible for big sales revenues. They disliked it because the channel put a lot of pressure on product price, and sometimes no profit was ensured for manufacturers.

After trials and errors, Dong Mingzhu's innovative sales model for Gree produced a magic weapon that would allow Gree to win the market. Dong Mingzhu said: "Sales companies and Gree Stores were driving engines for Gree's progressive development. Gree created and enhanced cohesion with the distributors, eschewed price fluctuation because of disorderly market competition, and directed all resources to scientific research."

In Dong Mingzhu's opinion, the model of Gree Stores bore similarities and disparities with Gome's chain stores. Gree Stores could be perceived as chain stores like Gome. The difference was that they only sold the Gree brand of air conditioners, in a specified and fine manner, while the variety of brands in Gome was large and comprehensive. In terms of size and scale, Gree Stores couldn't attract as many customers as chain stores like Gome. Gree took different measures to compensate for this disadvantage and engaged in competition.

Dong Mingzhu said proudly that thousands of suppliers and distributors congregated on either side of Gree's supply chain. After 20 years of development, Gree had built more than 30,000 retail outlets, and 20,000 Gree Stores, which were weaved into a sales network covering cities, counties and small towns. By advantage of its sales channels, Gree took over 44% of the market share in the countryside. Among all sales that year, Gree Stores contributed over 90%.

INVESTING IN MANUFACTURING CENTRES

On 26 March, Gree's tenth global manufacturing base was opened in the Ningxiang Economic Zone in Hunan. A new Gree air conditioner city was going to be built soon, which was a new benchmark for automation and intelligence in air conditioner manufacturing. With the introduction of the world's leading technology, management and personnel, Hunan would become another growth pole of China's household appliance industry, after the first three in the Pearl River Delta, Yangtze River Delta and Jiaodong Peninsula.

Gree founded the strategic partnership with Ningxiang in 2010, and invested 300 million RMB to build an eco-friendly remanufacturing base and regional sales centre in central China. With Gree's green remanufacturing base in production, it could recycle as many as 1.2 million discarded household appliances each year, a new record in the renewable industry in Hunan, and even in China. The regional sales centre in Gree would cover services including logistics, warehousing, sales and service in the central region of China. It would become the largest regional logistics centre, with multiple functions in trade and exhibitions, logistics and distribution, promotion and information exchange, and industry cultivation.

In October 2013, Gree officially signed a contract for investment in its tenth global manufacturing base with Ningxiang's Economic Zone administration. The project went smoothly after that. The total investment was more than 5 billion RMB. On about 2,000 acres of land, Gree was going to build the biggest household appliances manufacturing base, which encompassed the entire process of research, manufacture and sales in business and household air conditioners, air-source water heaters and water purifiers. The projected annual output could amount to up to 35 billion RMB, with a tax revenue of more than 1.5 billion RMB and employment of 10,000 new employees. It was a big event for the economic and social development in Hunan and the expansion of Gree Electric. It was also a big event for the development of China's national industry.

Gree's manufacturing base in Ninxiang would develop a new growth pole of the household appliance industry in Hunan. The chairwoman and president of Gree, Dong Mingzhu, said the investment in Ningxiang was a deliberate movement in the conquest of the world by Gree. It was as essential and resolute as Dong Mingzhu's book implied.

As a specified air conditioner manufacturer, Gree strove to provide air conditioners with advanced technology and high quality to global customers. Before the set-up of the manufacturing base in Ningxiang, Gree owned nine other manufacturing bases in Zhuhai, Chongqing, Hefei, Zhengzhou, Wuhan, Wuhu, Brazil, Pakistan and Vietnam, with an employment of 80,000 people, and developed more than 7,000 different products with 400 series and 20 categories for different needs of customers. Gree owned more than 9,000 technology patents, among which 2,500 were new inventions. Many independently developed products were ahead of the global industry, and new technology inventions filled the gap in China and rewrote the history of air conditioners.

In September 2003, the analysis of more than 120 Chinese public companies, undertaken by renowned investment bank Credit Suisse First Boston, named Gree as "one of the 12 Chinese companies of most investment value", the only household appliance company on the list. In June 2004, Gree Electric was listed as "one of the 50 Chinese Companies with Most Development Potential" for the sixth year, again the only household appliance company listed. In 2005, Gree took over LG's position as the biggest global air conditioner company, a supreme glory for the Chinese national industry.

Dong Mingzhu started as a sales associate at Gree in 1990, and held the positions of chairwoman at Gree Group, and chairwoman and president of Gree Electric all together for 23 years. For a long time, Dong Mingzhu was the equivalent of Gree Electric, and spokesperson of Gree. Gree had entered the 'Dong Mingzhu Age'.

Dong Mingzhu emphasized that Gree would remain determined on the path of specialized manufacturing. She thought there was no glass ceiling for the industry. Gree would keep persisting in the big air conditioning industry, which included central air conditioning and refrigerating systems. She said: "The company may go through bankruptcy, but the industry would never go bankrupt. We need to hone our capacity in the difficult settings and make achievements in it."

PURSUING
THE GOAL OF
INTERNATIONALIZATION

Gree is an influential global brand with business in more than 100 countries and regions worldwide. The manufacturing capacity is 60 million units of household air conditioners, and 5.5 million business units. Since 2005, the sales revenue of Gree has been leading the world for nine years. The user base is more than 300 million.

As early as 1993, Gree Electric had been exploring internationalization. In that year, Gree received contracts for manufacturing orders from Panasonic, Daikin and other famous global brands because of its lower cost and evident quality. The exports grew exponentially. Gree's products were even sold in Japan, the birthplace of traditional manufacturing giants in the household electronics industry. This marked the start of Gree's products entering the mainstream global market.

At the end of 1994, Gree got the first CE authorization from the European Union, and opened itself to the European market. Starting in 1995, Gree took the leading place in sales revenue and market shares in the domestic market. In 1997, Gree paid off all its bank loans and established a regional sales company with assets and a brand as the link, which paved a new path for sales in addition to the big chain stores of Gome and Suning.

In 1998, after inspection of the overseas market, after much deliberation, Gree's management team decided to start the internationalization and expansion to new markets. In October 1998, Gree entered Brazil and sold Gree products in all big supermarkets in Brazil. In March 1999, Gree set up a special committee to research the feasibility of having a manufacturing plant in Brazil. On 6 June 2001, Gree invested more than 3 million USD in the Manaus Economic Free Zone and established Gree Electric (Brazil) Co. Ltd., which had an annual manufacturing capacity of 200,000 units. In 2006, Gree Electric established its second overseas manufacturing base in Pakistan, with a capacity of 100,000 units. In 2007, Gree invested in another manufacturing base in the Singapore Industrial Park in Ho Chi Minh City, Vietnam, which was put into production in April 2008.

The manufacturing capacity of Gree grew exponentially since its foundation. It had become the largest professional air conditioner manufacturing base in the world, with products exported to more than 200 countries and regions in Europe, Asia, Africa, South America and North America. In regard to brand awareness and product quality, Gree was the world leader.

Dong Mingzhu emphasized the engagement of international competition as an inevitable means of Gree's development. Globalization was not just about low costs, but achieving the optimal allocation of resources. Dong Mingzhu believed that in the new economic situation, the advantages of allocation of resources were revealed. With modern information technology and logistics networks, as well as the integration of the global economy, resource allocation had been extended from a factory, a region or a country to the whole world.

Dong Mingzhu said that internationalization was based on the rules and regulations of international competition, which emphasized the product. She believed the company must own the core technology to not be defeated. So far, Gree had more than 5,000 R&D staff, and more than 300 laboratories. Gree had acquired more than 1,431 patents in the last three years. On average, about nine new inventions came out every week. Gree owned the most patents in the air conditioning industry and had the highest investment in scientific research. It was one of the few Chinese air conditioner enterprises independent of foreign technology support.

Dong Mingzhu said that Gree didn't place a cap on innovation and R&D investment, which contributed to its growing brand awareness in the world. Gree air conditioners won contracts from an airport in India, the South African World Cup stadium, the Sochi Winter Olympics Shopping

Centre, the Beijing Olympic Media Village and other major international projects. The lucrative orders came one after another. Gree also achieved the highest air conditioner sales revenue in the world for eight consecutive years.

Dong Mingzhu explained, "The internationalization of Gree is not simply about the sales figures, revenue or profit. What's more valuable is global brand awareness and to provide good products to global consumers." Dong Mingzhu emphasized that technological support for internationalization was needed.

Every step of Gree's process of internationalization was a manifestation of its resolution and strong capacity. In more than 20 years, Gree had developed into the world's largest air conditioning manufacturing enterprise through independent technological innovations. Its core technology kept abreast of leading American and Japanese enterprises, and surpassed them sometimes. Its technological innovation and breakthroughs in many fields made it an air conditioner manufacturing leader in the world.

EMPHASIZING INNOVATION FOR FURTHER DEVELOPMENT

On 7 November 2005, the Ministry of Construction, the National Development and Reform Commission, the Chinese Institute of Refrigeration, China Association of Refrigeration Technology and other authoritative organizations jointly organized an assessment of scientific and technological achievements. The latest Gree models of ultra-low temperature digital central air conditioning systems were considered to have achieved leading international status.

Looking back at the history of air conditioners in the last century, the United States and Japan had dominated the core technology. The world's first air conditioner was invented in the United States. After World War II, Japanese enterprises innovated in split air conditioners and outperformed American brands. However, the US enterprises had an absolute leading edge in central air conditioning. Zhu Jianghong believed that Chinese enterprises must rely on their own efforts to catch up with Japanese and American brands, rather than counting on their charity for technology.

In order to continuously improve technology and innovation, Gree committed more than 3% of its revenue to technology R&D annually, which was the highest investment in technology in the Chinese air conditioning industry. By 2012, Gree had formed its own research team, and three fundamental research institutions, namely the Institute of Refrigeration Technology, the Electrical and Mechanical Technology Research Institute and the Institute of Household Appliances Technology, to focus on the research of cutting edge technologies and long-term development. In addition, Gree had more than 300 specialized laboratories for research and experiment on the newly developed products in various circumstances.

Dong Mingzhu said that Gree owned more than 6,000 domestic and foreign technology patents, including 1,300 patents on new inventions. Gree had developed more than 7,000 different products with 400 series and 20 categories for consumer groups. Gree had more than 5,000 R&D personnel, including some foreign experts. More than 90% of R&D personnel held a bachelor's degree. Gree created a culture of respecting talent and technology, set up awards for scientific and technological progress, and rewarded those who made big contributions. The award bonus was as high as 1 million yuan.

Dong Mingzhu said that without innovation, a business didn't have a soul; without a good quality product, the enterprise was grotesque. To pursue the world's cutting-edge air conditioning technology, Gree built the world's largest air conditioning R&D centre, and owned more than 220 professional laboratories to test thermal balance, noise and reliability, which led the world in quantity, size and technology development. In addition, Gree established a large refrigeration research institute to apply for the patents on its technology. Gree led the world in its product categories.

In independent innovation, Gree implemented the 'three-step' pragmatic approach. First, it implemented the 'market-centring' strategy to concentrate on the development of the products that were urgently needed in the market and accumulate competitive advantages in cooling capacity, energy efficiency, quiet operation and longevity. Second, it implemented the strategy of 'filling the domestic gap' to break the foreign monopoly and to achieve independent R&D, especially in important subfields. Third, it implemented the strategy of 'surpassing international standards' to develop advanced new products and lead the international industry.

Gree Electric's annual report from 2013 showed that the total revenue was 120.03 billion RMB, with a year-on-year increase of 19.9%; the net profit for shareholders was 10.813 billion RMB, with an increase of 46.53%, the highest growth in history. According to its public financial reports, Gree was the first household electrical appliance enterprise in China with an annual net profit of more than 10 billion RMB.

According to some statistics, Gree had more than 5,000 R&D personnel, two state-level technology centres, four research academies, 28 research institutes, and more than 500 laboratories. Investment in R&D surpassed 4 billion RMB in 2012 and 2013, far beyond the level of international counterparts. Gree owned more than 9,000 domestic and foreign patents, of which more than 2,500 were patents on new inventions. In 2013 alone, Gree applied for more than 2,700 patents, about eight patents a day on average.

Dong Mingzhu appeared in the list of Global Top 50 Businesswomen in Fortune magazine for the ninth time in 2013.

Dong Mingzhu has said proudly that Gree's air conditioners have been exported to more than 100 countries and regions, and have entered the mainstream market in the US. Gree has built main sales channels in those countries and is recognized by mainstream consumer groups. Gree has won recognition and respect through its independent innovation.

APPENDICES:

SPEECHES BY DONG MINGZHU

BE HARSH
ON YOURSELF

On 20 July 2013, Dong Mingzhu gave a speech, titled "Be Harsh on Yourself", on the CCTV television show *Voice*. The full transcript is below:

I can say very proudly that Gree was a specialized enterprise that only manufactured air conditioners. In 20 years, our sales revenue soared from 20 million to 100 billion, and from 20,000 units to 40 million units annually. How did we achieve this? It's not only me, but all Gree employees; we are harsh on ourselves and make constant improvements to the product.

When I applied for the job to be a sales associate at Gree, I didn't understand a thing about air conditioners, to be honest. The first big problem I encountered was a debt of more than 400,000 left by another associate. Many people told me, "Dong Mingzhu, it was not your business. You were not responsible for that." I said, "I am an employee of Gree. Since I have taken this position, I need to be responsible to the company." I spent more than 40 days collecting this debt. I showed up at the door of the client's office every day and tracked him down every place he went. Finally he agreed to give back the products, but disappeared again on the scheduled day. I talked to his employees with empathy and reason and put them in my shoes. They were moved by me and promised to tell me when their boss showed up. On the second day, I showed up. I was emotional and decided to carry out the products myself. I didn't care if the air conditioners were heavy. I would pull them to the truck with all my strength. I was afraid that he would stop me, even after I loaded the air conditioners on the truck. I waited until the engine started to tell him that I would never do business with him again in my lifetime. My tears welled up. I cried. It was so hard to collect debt.

Many people didn't understand me in this. "It was not your personal belongings. Why did you bother?" I believed I needed to maintain my principles and be responsible to my company, as long as I was an employee of this company. After that, people said to me that I should go to the headquarters and become the director of the sales department. I was a sales associate at that time and could earn more than a million for a deal. A manager could only make a few thousand at that time. I thought it was better to be a sales associate. On second thought, however, I realized that if the company fell apart, I couldn't survive, no matter how capable I was.

I will tell you two stories of how I benefited from being harsh to myself after I became the director of the sales department. The first one is about my brother. At that time, we had a prime season and an off-season for air conditioner sales. In the prime season, all distributors wanted more stock and supplies. Someone approached my brother, and bribed him with 20,000–30,000 RMB if he managed to get a million RMB worth of air conditioners for them. My brother was excited about this deal and called me, saying that he would be in Zhuhai in two days. I asked why he was coming to Zhuhai all of a sudden. He told me he was coming for air conditioner supplies. I asked: "You are not a distributor. How come you are coming for the supply?" He told me he commissioned 20,000 to 30,000 for a million worth of products.

I told him not to come and hung up on him. I immediately asked the distributor if he went to my brother for more supplies. He thought I was persuaded and joyfully admitted it. I told him his initial supply was suspended because of his misdeed. He couldn't understand my decision. In his opinion, Gree lost nothing; we could just provide the air conditioner supplies at the usual price, and my brother could get some money for it. It was good for the business and my family.

Why didn't I do it? He couldn't figure it out and went to ask my brother if we were biological siblings. My brother couldn't understand me either. He thought that what he had asked was neither illegal nor immoral, just a request to use my power to help the family and give them a chance to make money. Why didn't I do it? I told him that my power wasn't meant to serve him or myself. That distributor promised to me on paper that he would never approach my brother again. After I resumed his supply, he made more than 70 million RMB in sales that year. If those went through my brother on the 2% he had offered, my brother could have made more than a million that year. If I did that, my brother would make a fortune, but how would other distributors view Gree Electric? Would they still be committed to the market expansion, or just trying to pull strings?

My brother didn't come to understand me until 2001, when he truly understood why I was so harsh on myself. This is what we should do with power in our hands.

What's the second story about? When I became the director of the sales department, I realized more problems plagued our company. In the prime season, everyone had power in their hands. Even the porter asked for a box of bottled water in return for carrying the air conditioners to the truck, let alone those who wrote invoices. It developed to the extremes, with every distributor sending people gifts. Whoever sent the biggest gifts would have air conditioners delivered to them first. You could imagine the vitality of our company in that state. Just now, the host mentioned that many enterprises that shot advertisements starring Jackie Chan collapsed. It had nothing to do with Jackie Chan. It was because the enterprise didn't have an effective management system.

When I started to work as the director of the sales department, many people said I went from easy-going to tough. How tough was I? I initiated the regulation that all female workers couldn't wear accessories like earrings or rings, nor wear long hair. Those who insisted on long hair needed to wear a hair bun, or they were not allowed to be at work.

Many people may wonder why I was so strict. It was because we were a very loose department at that time, and I needed to build the idea of a group in them. I made another regulation that no one was allowed to eat snacks or gossip together during work time. You were here to work. If you had nothing to do, just read a book. Some office workers didn't take my words seriously. They thought I was just bluffing. One day when I inspected, maybe it was only five seconds away from quitting time, but I saw some employees eating snacks in the office. I fined them on the spot. They made excuses that the snack was brought by someone else, and it would be too unkind to say no. I said I would fine each of them 50 yuan and fine the person who brought the food 100 yuan. The one who brought the snack was from a very poor family, and the office worker only made 800 yuan, so 100 yuan was a big sum. I waited until after work and gave him 100 yuan from my pocket. I told him, "I didn't return your fine. The fine was taken by the finance department. This is my help to you because of your financial situation." The punishment made our employees aware of company rules and regulations.

When I became the manager, some employees went on strike. In the management meeting, someone complained that those employees were unreasonable and hard to manage. I disagreed. Our employees were nice and good people. They were subjective to our management. They did what our managers did. The root of those bad behaviours was in our management team. So the first thing I did when I became the manager was to rectify management executives' behaviour. Before that, many people wondered, "Dong Mingzhu was a good saleswoman, but could she manage the company well?" After that conference on regulations on management behaviour, they knew how good I was at this. They bargained with me to have a fresh start and leave the past in the past. I said no, because they had encroached on a state-owned asset and used their power to maximize their personal gain. They hurt our employees, and it was not allowed.

When I was the general manager, I cleaned up the management team and heard the voices of front-line workers. I found that the manager mailbox was always placed at the door of the factory manager's office. Who dared to put a complaint in it? The factory manager would know who had filed the complaint about him and fire them. No one dared to file a complaint. What should I do? I placed a large number of manager mailboxes everywhere, in the canteen or bathroom, or other unobvious places, and received as many as 700 complaint letters at the peak time. We identified our problems from those 700 complaint letters and built up a good management team. This is how harsh I was to my team.

Many people asked if all my devotion to Gree was worth it. I thought it was worth it, because people would connect me with Gree everywhere in the world. Once I went through a security check in Taiwan, and a security worker asked if I was Dong Mingzhu. I said yes with a smile. He told me he used a Gree air conditioner. Can you buy this kind of connection and respect with money? No. To pursue your value of life, you can't just see the short-term benefit. Don't live for money. I believe the value of life lies not in wealth, but your conscience of examining yourself. I tell my employees on many occasions that other people are considered successful by making a lot of money. I don't believe in that. I am very happy because I have empowered other people to become millionaires and billionaires. I think my value is achieved by society's approval.

When I was 12 years old, our teacher took us to swim. I didn't like it. I thought the movements were ugly. The teacher talked me through it. He said, "You are a big girl. Why can't you do that?" I was motivated. My teacher introduced me to three coaches who had swam across the Yangtze River and asked them to coach me. They were at home in water. They gave me a stick and asked me to wait in the water while they swam a round trip. I almost drowned. The water was just this deep, but I fell down and couldn't get up in the river. Some other people rescued me.

You may think I would have stayed away from water from then on, but I became more determined to learn swimming, because if I couldn't swim, I was prone to that danger always. I had the same resilience in biking. Once I almost ran into a bus when I was riding home. I was cycling very fast and leaned backwards to dodge the bus, and then I fell to the ground. My first response was to get up immediately, without dusting off my pants, because I was embarrassed, but I never refrained from riding a bike again. I didn't. I learned from the experience and kept practising.

I have another story that may not fall into the category of being harsh on yourself. I have never picked up my son from school. Once I drove past his school right at the time when school was finished. I wanted to stop and pick him up, but I didn't. I made him walk home. He was home late that night, and I asked him why. He told me he had waited for the non-air-conditioned bus to save one kuai for fare and ended up waiting for more than half an hour. Do we really need that one kuai for life? No. I was harsh on him, so he learned to struggle in the difficult conditions. He has graduated from college and works for another company. He said, "Mom, you started from scratch, so could I." He worked for a monthly salary of 5,000, but he was happy and enjoyed the process. It was a great comfort to me.

This is all I want to tell you here. I hope you can realize that only struggle will add value to your life. This applies to me. That's all I want to tell you. Thank you!

GREE
ALMOST DIED

On the afternoon of 22 April 2016, Dong Mingzhu went back to her home town, Nanjing, to attend the 2016 Innovative Enterprise Development Summit of Businessmen from Suzhu, and the Golden Jasmine Award Ceremony. Dong Mingzhu gave the speech below on her management experience at Gree, a Fortune 500 enterprise.

Good afternoon. I am very honoured to be here today. Jiangning in Nanjing is my home town. I wondered who this Golden Jasmine Award would go to, and I didn't expect it would be me. Thank you so much.

In 2003, each city wanted to have a Fortune 500

enterprise in the region. Many people thought the acquisition of Gree by a foreign company was secure, and we could have a Fortune 500 enterprise in Zhuhai in that way.

How much did they offer at that time? They offered 900 million RMB based on the net assets of Gree, and they offered me 80 million RMB a year for my salary. It was so tempting. Why didn't I just accept it? I told them I wouldn't sell Gree to them. I said: "You are in the Fortune 500 list today. Maybe I will make that list tomorrow."

I fulfilled this dream today. If I sold Gree for 900 million, how could I pay more than 15 billion in taxes each year to our country? Would Gree still be a renowned global brand? When we turned down the offer, we were faced with the difficulties that may have courted our own ruin. I went to the provincial government to meet Zhang Dezhang, who was the secretary of the Guangdong provincial party committee at that time. I argued there was no rhyme or reason to let another national brand extinguish, like Zhonghua toothpaste, which was still run by our people and used our materials, but the brand didn't belong to us anymore.

In the government report this year, the prime minister made it very clear that only struggle could lead to fortune. The meaning is fundamental. We can not rely on heaven or earth or help from others. A successful man always contributes to others' courses and makes others happy.

In the household appliances industry, Gree is the only enterprise that hasn't entered into the real estate market, which took an important part in the development of the Chinese economy and was very lucrative. Some places even invited us for investment. We turned all of them down, because we needed to work for the entire economy and be responsible for the development of the manufacturing industry.

Do we need people like Ma Yun? Yes, but we don't need many of them. We need many people like Dong Mingzhu, who represent the backbone of the Chinese economy, a strong manufacturing industry.

Looking back at our development history, we made huge achievements in a short time. What competitiveness do we possess and what do we lack? We lack in innovation. In the process of Gree's development of more than 20 years, we realized what our pursuit was.

In 1991, our sales revenue was only 100 million RMB, as you can see on this chart. We had sales revenue of 100 million RMB in 1991, and that's risen to 140 billion RMB right now, with a profit of more than 10 billion RMB. Our development had two milestones, and the first was in 1995. In 1995, our sales revenue doubled, from 400 million to 800 million, which was when we started to make profits. If we hadn't started to make profits in 1995, we may have shut down in 1997.

The second was in 2001, when our sales revenue broke 10 billion RMB, and we launched a rectification of management behaviours. How many problems did we find? The first one was the abuse of management power for private gains. We always associate corruption with government officials, but it can happen anywhere with business dealings.

When I was appointed the director of the sales department and went to work at Gree headquarters, I found a series of personnel issues that disturbed the development of Gree.

The general manager at that time was from Guangxi and took a few of his people to Gree. He was often not aware of the conduct of his subordinates, who assumed his authority as their own. Those people didn't have any titles, but even some deputy managers dreaded dealing with them.

When we have personal considerations in a business matter or decision, we may choose different methods. If we all bear personal considerations, do you think the enterprise and company could still develop? I don't think so.

When I came back to the headquarters, I had the biggest sales record, and people called me the queen of sales. I told others that my achievements came from my sacrifice. When I was a sales associate in Nanjing, no one knew that was my home town. I kept a professional distance from distributors, but I worked very hard to expand the market for them. So I contributed one tenth of Gree's 400 million RMB in revenue that year.

To become the director of the sales department could have been a loss to me personally. I could make more than 1 million RMB as a sales associate, but only 100,000 as director. However, I decided to take the position and be responsible. I started the regulation with those few subordinates of the deputy manager. If they could get around the regulation, the regulation couldn't be implemented in the company.

I kept an eye on them. I made a rule as the director of the sales department that without notice from the finance department that their payment was received, no delivery should be arranged to distributors. But one of our manager's subordinates broke this rule and ordered the delivery before payment. I fined him 100 yuan out of his salary, which was only 800 yuan at that time. I made an announcement of this punishment across the company and degraded his salary scale. I was asked to the manager's office the next day and asked to explain the situation. I told the manager about this person's misconduct and my wish to dismiss him if I had the power.

The manager was not happy with my decision, but he was open-minded. The sales revenue was 2.8 million RMB that year under my leadership, and he didn't downgrade my position or fire me, but assigned me to be the manager of the Gree Sales Company, because my dealing with that matter solved the fundamental problem of setting up rules in the company. The matter could have been big or small, but it was impactful at that time.

Because of that person's connection with our manager, he was mobilized to work in another department. A few years later, I was promoted to manage the department he was in. I told him to watch out. I was not against him personally, but he could break the company's rules as the subordinate of our manager.

There were about 400 to 500 air conditioner companies at that time, but few of them have survived until today. What's the reason for that? Some may say the competition was fierce, but I attributed it to the lack of management and regulation. If the head of the company couldn't clearly see that, it predicted disaster. I set up the regulations when I became the director, but many people didn't understand me, because I beat against the current while they went with the stream. However, if it were not for those regulations, Gree would have collapsed long ago. The biggest problem in Gree at that time was the lack of profits. When I had a profit of 10 million RMB on our account, we borrowed 50 million RMB in loans. I worked on that matter for all of

1995 and implemented new regulations. If we recovered all of our debt, we didn't even need the loans from the bank. The matter was completely solved in 1997, when we reversed the situation completely. Gree had assets worth more than 100 billion RMB, and we haven't applied for any loans from the bank since 1997. That was the advantage of rules and regulation.

To cultivate a new culture, you may offend some people who are beneficiaries of the previous system. Once you start a new system and a new culture, they become your opponents and look for your shortcomings.

Selling air conditioners was a lucrative business at that time. A batch of deliveries may have induced about 200,000 to 300,000 sales, so the delivery time mattered to distributors during the prime season. Chinese people have a culture of connections. No one in my company knew my home town, but a distributor was very capable and found my brother.

My brother called me that day and told me he would come to Zhuhai. I was very busy because of the prime season and asked him not to come. He said he was not coming to visit me, but to get a batch of air conditioners for a distributor, who offered him a 20,000 to 30,000 yuan commission on the delivery of 1 million worth of air conditioners.

I was appalled and agitated at that time, because I threw myself into my career at Gree. From 1995, when I was first promoted, to 2007, I was exhausted and hospitalized in November each year, but the problems were so complicated at Gree and it needed my devotion. Even in the hospital, I met some distributors during the day, which people dubbed as expert outpatient service. I needed to talk to each distributor individually, even if they were from the same province. You could see I was in an abominable environment.

My brother was pleased with this offer, but when I heard about his commission, I hung up on him. My brother and I didn't see each other for more than 20 years after that. He wrote me a letter to announce that he didn't have a sister. I was too cruel. Why was he so upset? Because I called the distributor who approached him and suspended his supply for half a month during the prime season until he promised never to deal with my brother. He was shocked by my forceful response and asked my brother if I was his real sister, which upset my brother even more.

I knew my brother was disappointed in this matter, but we needed to make deliberate decisions in our choices. In my brother's argument, he said he could have asked someone else who worked for me for this favour. It was nothing illegal or immoral. Why did I turn him down? Other people would help their families with their fortune, but I could not even do him a favour when I was the director of the sales department.

The distributor didn't understand me either. He said they went through connections to get supplies all the time. This time he offered my brother a fortune, so why did I turn him down? He thought I was too aloof. This distributor is not working in the air conditioning industry anymore, but when we met, he still appreciated the profit margin I granted him, even though I had strict rules and regulations.

Therefore, Gree didn't fall apart in the collective resignation incident. We used our regulations to build an equal environment for the distributors and united other enterprises in our supply chain. Our revenue grew by seven times that year, and we outperformed Chunli to become the top air conditioner brand in the domestic market in 1996.

I am very proud that we just won two big international awards in the air conditioning industry, the equivalent of an Oscar for entertainment. Speaking of which, I will tell you another story. It is not a sordid story, but I will still tell you because I want to get the words off my chest. Many people say that I shouldn't speak like this as a public figure, but I believe public figures need to speak the truth. If we dare not speak the truth, there would be no value in us.

An advertisement from another brand highlighting one degree of electricity consumption every night fooled many people, those consumers who didn't understand the technology. The court ruled for compensation, and the industrial and commercial bureau announced it as false advertisement. It changed the wording to as low as one degree of electricity consumption every night. What does it mean? If it is 25°C outside, we don't need to turn on air conditioners.

No one pointed out this malpractice except me. I pointed it out. They tried to win the award for progressive technology with this lie. I was completely against them. If they managed to win the award, how would others in the world view the science and technology development level in China? Other people said it was not decent of me to say that the Midea brand was a thief. They questioned my personality, but my behaviour promoted the development of technology in China.

I told everyone that Midea was a thief, but they didn't sue me for slander. They dared not, because the court ordered them to issue two million RMB in compensation to Gree. If they didn't steal Gree's patent, why did the court order them to provide compensation? They even stole our trademark. Why couldn't I call them a thief?

One day, in a meeting, I said that some enterprises didn't cultivate their own talents. They relied on bringing in people from other enterprises, which was another act of stealing. They would send some people to poach our employees at the gate of our company. Not only Chinese enterprises did this. Some foreign companies were involved too. If you pay me, I can develop my talents for you. I cultivated talent for a dozen years, and you stole him from me with a high salary. How can we keep innovation for the made-in-China brands?

I beat them up that day. They said I had violated the law by hitting people. I told them to sue, but they dared not. After this incident, some reporters interviewed Midea for their response. They said they were like a good husband, never shouting or fighting back. They got shot even lying down.

I am not fighting against Midea, but against all bad practices in the industry. Only by fighting all behaviours that harm the interests of customers can the made-in-China brands be strong in the world.

In the government report, the government attached great importance to the development of the manufacturing industry by regulating patent infringement acts, cracking down on counterfeit and shoddy products, and improving product quality. The State Council just issued another document a few days ago, which mentioned the phenomenon of many people buying toilet seats and rice cookers from Japan. This is the first year of the 13th Five-Year Plan. We prioritize product quality even without government regulations.

The government report brought up the idea of craftsmanship. What's craftsmanship? We always place emphasis on the craftsman, which was wrong from the beginning. How could craftsmanship relate to people at each post in an enterprise? It's about the endeavour for perfection in each detail. Management level need craftsmanship and front-line workers need it too. Why do we always talk about Germany for craftsmanship, as if their products embody craftsmanship and Chinese products were the equivalent of cheap and shabby products? Our understanding of craftsmanship is wrong. It is the courage to challenge the status quo and the spirit of sacrifice.

In the incident involving panic buying of toilet seats and rice cookers from Japan, I said publicly that I was proud that Gree honoured the manufacturing industry by making the best air conditioners in the world. It is impossible for you to find a better air conditioner brand. Even the People's Great Hall is equipped with Gree air conditioners. The nuclear industry base uses Gree's brand too, and it requires a temperature of -40°C. Our technology was our support. I say at every occasion that you won't have any complaint about our air conditioners, and you will regret it if you don't choose Gree. This is my confidence, my promise.

Qin Shuo asked me one day in Beijing where Gree had the best sales revenue. I know everything about Gree like the back of my hand. I told him in the Middle East. He agreed. He had just come back from the Middle East. He said he had been to the mall and had seen that all the air conditioners there were of the Gree brand.

Qin Shuo was proud of Gree too, and asked the shop owners why they chose Gree. They told him that they had hot weather seven months a year, when the temperature was between 35°C and 40°C. Only Gree worked in those extreme conditions. How proud was I when heard this? I think you should applaud not for me or Gree, but for Chinese-made brands.

What's the core of competitiveness? It's innovation. Without innovation, there is no core competitiveness. You can bring in the technology, but it's not your innovation. That's why Gree has seven research institutes, and more than 8,000 R&D personnel.

The culture of Gree is the culture of innovation. We instil this value in each employee and inspire him to perfect his post. This returns to the point I made just now. Management staff and other employees need to focus on their own duties. I think about ways to make employees live a better life, and we have a strict standard for their work at the same time.

When I became the president of Gree, I went over the personnel list of the company, and found more than 200 senior employees who started to work for Gree in the 1980s and still worked for Gree. Those who started at Gree didn't leave. They were from different places and still didn't have a permanent residence in Zhuhai. I asked a favour from the government to grant them permanent residence in Zhuhai, so they could receive their pension after retirement.

Many people didn't understand why I did this for them, since they were going to retire soon and had nothing to do with Gree. They were wrong. If we held that attitude for those who worked at Gree for more than 20 years, how could young people still have faith in Gree? A lot of people don't ask for high salaries, but they want the security, the platform to grow and the chance to prove themselves. I talked with the city government, and they agreed to grant them permanent residence in Zhuhai so they could have a nice life after retirement. This was what we should have done, and what we did touched a lot of people, who are now even more confident and loyal to Gree.

We just built more than a thousand apartments for Gree employees in the university town of Zhuhai. You can live in those apartments for free after a few years of working for Gree. You can move out if you can afford better housing. As long as you don't have a house, you can enjoy this benefit. This is what I just said: consider your employees' needs. Don't wait until they make requests. We need to consider those things for them and help make their lives better. What's more important than to provide a platform for young people to grow and achieve?

I have the most power in the company, but the least as well. I am the chairwoman and president. People think this is the age of my dictatorship, but I think this is when I have the least power. We all have the same goal at Gree. Anyone can take any position if it helps us to get close to this goal. Gree Electric has diversified its development and owns several famous brands. We want to create a positive vibe for Chinese manufacturing with all the brands we have. This is the goal of Gree.

We don't pursue profits now, but will strive to build a strong national enterprise. This is our value and our dream. We export our products to different places in the world and build manufacturing bases around the world, but not to take advantage of cheap resources or underdeveloped markets in Vietnam or the Philippines. That's not our goal. We export to the US and Europe as well.

We need to build the image of made-in-China, and bring made-in-China products to the world. Our pursuit of craftsmanship could have prevented the incident of panic buying of toilet seats in Japan.

People think we only own a few brands after so many years. We produce cell phones, too. People say I am fighting against Xiaomi. But Xiaomi isn't worth my fight, because it would lose eventually. Why? Because Xiaomi contracts manufacturers, and we make cell phones ourselves. Many people endeavour in speculation, but we toil in the basic aspects. They think manufacturing is a loss in this age, but I can turn meagre profits to exorbitant profits. Our manufacturing capacity is our base and our power to make us smile.

I want to tell you the story of our solar air conditioner. Does it meet the national standard? We meet the international standard. Some other products may claim they meet the standard too.

In 2012, when I was the chairwoman of Gree, I went to a product quality evaluation agency. Someone received me warmly and assured me they would support me. I asked how they would support me? Was this by giving my products the stamp of qualification even if they didn't meet the standard? Why are made-in-China products despised in the world? Those agencies are partly responsible. They may do a favour to enterprises to let them pass quality evaluation, but the market won't agree with their evaluation.

So when I talked to him, I asked him for a favour, to adhere to the most strident standard for our products, to pick bones with our products. Even for a minor problem, he needed to return the product to the factory. He was confused. In his working experience of a dozen years, I was the first manager he met to have this requirement. I told him that he might let our products pass the evaluation today, even if they were a little away from the standard. The bar would keep decreasing, and our products would decay to the shoddy products that could only be sold at a cheap price. Why did our domestic customers buy those shoddy products at a cheap price? I advocate no buying of those products, because if there were some support for them in the market, their standard would keep falling.

I initiated an alliance of "made-in-China, loved by the world" last year. We are going to have the second summit this year in the Great People's Hall, to involve more entrepreneurs to crack down on shoddy products and make a common target for attack towards all who were involved, no matter who was behind them in support. We are not scared. We will persist.

What prompted us to research solar air conditioning? In 2012, when I attended the conference of the NPC, many people suggested that we develop air purifiers to counter the air pollution. Should air purifiers be developed? Yes, because air pollution is so serious. Another thought just dawned on me, that the air conditioners we developed were detrimental to the environment and very energy consuming. Was it a sad story if our products cost people their health?

Air conditioner usage accounts for 30% of electricity consumption in China, or even more. I thought solar would be better for energy consumption. If we cut 30% of energy consumption, air pollution could be reduced by half. I wondered if there were nonelectric air conditioners. Some people said there were not. I said we could use solar energy.

They said solar energy was to generate electricity, and air conditioners consumed electricity. How to make it work was a challenge. I told them the value was in the challenge. They needed to research that. I would grant them 100 million

RMB or 200 million RMB and wouldn't hold them responsible if nothing came out of their research. They worked two years and were finally successful. Solar air conditioners sell well in the Middle East because they have abundant sunshine. In the summer the sunlight is strong, and the air conditioner is used all the time, but uses no electricity. This technology is disruptive.

The Chinese president has advertised for Gree air conditioners. He told me when he visited foreign countries, other national leaders told him that Gree was great, except for being too quiet, and customers forgot to turn it off all the time. We became more meticulous after we heard this remark. We need to ensure the quiet operations to not discredit this remark. It inspired us to make the best product to the extreme.

The second generation of Gree solar air conditioners was launched, which could store the electricity generated by sunlight for use at night. We did the math and found the product cost would be covered this way in four years, which was super beneficial for customers, as well as for saving energy and environmental protection. This is why we encouraged innovation, to make made-in-China become innovated-in-China.

The time of my speech is almost over, and the host has just reminded me of the time. However, I still have a lot to share with everyone. I welcome you to Zhuhai to discuss marketing, technology, management or talent cultivation with me. We can reflect on our experiences that have formed our own management system, which is extremely effective with regard to quality control.

The cost of screws for Gree in 2012 was 70 million RMB. It was reduced to 20 million RMB last year, despite more production. This is the benefit of management. Good management enhances the competitiveness of enterprises.

That's all of my speech today. Just a moment, I have to make an advertisement. I want to show you our cell phone, which will be launched on the market at the end of April or the beginning of May. We sell the cell phone separately, but in the future we will plan to give the cell phone for free when you buy Gree air conditioners.

I told the designer that our cell phones needed to be valuable to customers. The ultimate goal was that an idiot would know how to use it when they had it in their hand. That's the direction for Gree Electric development in the future: to provide more convenience to customers.

The competitiveness of Gree boils down to the high standard of product quality and technology and its international recognition. To achieve internationalization and a smart system in this age, Gree has its own smart equipment company.

I am over time again, but I am really happy. I think the significance of this meeting was to gather us all here to learn from each other. I promise here today that we will keep providing good products and are willing to share the experience. I learned a lot from you today, and I hope enterprises in Jiangzhu can achieve leading positions in China. Although I am in Guangdong now, I would like to come back home someday. Thank you all!

My most distinctive personality trait is that I fear no difficulties. We run into difficulties every day, and what really matters is how to perceive them. I am miserable without difficulties. The challenges enrich me.

The most difficult time for me was when other people didn't understand me. Someone once told me to be careful, that everyone was saying bad words behind my back. Whether I should keep going after hearing those words was the toughest decision I have ever had to make. I didn't shrink back because I would win eventually. What comforted me was that those people who hated me and said bad words about me recognize and appreciate my effort today. I need to be responsible to the past and future with my actions.

I cried once in November 1995, when I had a fever on a business trip and stayed in the hospital for 40 days. Doctors checked on my consciousness a few times and I worried how my son would fare if something happened to me. My biggest regret is for my mother and my son, but if I hadn't made the sacrifice, Gree wouldn't have achieved what it has today. For a woman, nothing is difficult if you dare to face it.